THE
LIFE AND DEATH
OF A
DRUID PRINCE

The Story of Lindow Man,
an Archaeological Sensation

ANNE ROSS and DON ROBINS

SUMMIT BOOKS

NEW YORK · LONDON · TORONTO
SYDNEY · TOKYO · SINGAPORE

SUMMIT BOOKS
Simon & Schuster Building
Rockefeller Center
1230 Avenue of the Americas
New York, New York 10020

Library of Congress Cataloging in Publication Data

Ross, Anne, Ph. D.
    The life and death of a Druid prince : the story of
Lindow Man, an archaeological sensation / Anne Ross
and Don Robins.
        p.   cm.
    "Originally published in Great Britain by Rider"—
T.p. verso.
    Includes bibliographical references (p.
    1. Lindow Man.   2. Iron age—England.
3. England—Antiquities.
I. Robins, Don.   II. Title.
GN780.22.G7R67   1989
936.2—dc20
ISBN 0–671–69536–3   90–9616
                                            CIP

Contents

AUTHORS' NOTE   7

PROLOGUE
    The Riddle of the Blackened Bread   9

ONE   The Silent Witness   15
TWO   Face to Face with a Druid   34
THREE Lovernios Revealed   53
FOUR   The Fox's Earth   60
FIVE   The Black Year   79
SIX   The Golden Twist   101

EPILOGUE
    The Triple Echo   128
APPENDIX ONE
    The Druids   130
APPENDIX TWO
    Celts and Germans   157

ACKNOWLEDGMENTS   168
BIBLIOGRAPHY   170
INDEX   174

Authors' Note

THE DISCOVERY of Lindow Man caused an initial flurry of excitement which soon abated after the uncovering of the grisly manner of
his death and the reporting of the initial research program by the
British Museum in 1986 (*The Body in the Bog*). No further general
work on the possible meaning of his life and death was published
until our article putting forward the Druid hypothesis came out
toward the end of 1987. The sheer lack of curiosity about the
antecedents of Lindow Man's life and death was one of the factors
that encouraged us to develop our Druid hypothesis further.

Originally, this book was planned as a new look at the Druids,
occasioned by our deduction that Lindow Man belonged to that
order. Its other, secondary, purpose was to explore the ritual
significance of his death against the background of the famous
Danish bog burials. In attempting these tasks we found ourselves
taking a hard look at a great many received opinions on these topics.
And as our investigations progressed we eventually began to piece
together a possible scenario which explained our deductions about
Lindow Man's life and death.

Our scholarly work on the Druids and the Danish bog bodies
viewed alongside the discovery of Lindow Man slowly developed a
new character as our research continued. It gradually turned into a
historical and archaeological detective story, and the original sub-
jects of the book were pushed further and further toward the
periphery as the pace of discovery quickened. Our insights into
druidism and the Danish sacrifices therefore now exist only as

7

appendages to the central detective story, though we hope to return to these themes and develop them fully at a later date. The ideas and opinions expressed in this book are, of course, our own responsibility. Many people have contributed through their work and in discussion, and among them we should like to express our particular gratitude to: Mr. T. J. Barron, Mr. T. Bruce Eve, Dr. A. B. Harris, Dr. G. Hillman, the late Mr. E. Holden, Dr. T. Holden, Mr. V. Horie, Miss C. M. Johns, Dr. D. Kenyon, Dr. D. Oduwole, Mr. M. Pinney, Miss V. Rigby, Dr. K. Sales and Mr. Anthony Myers Ward.

The late Pastor Knud Høgsbro Østergaard included among his wide researches the question of the Celtic element in the prehistory and history of Denmark, and generously offered valuable material for discussion. We are grateful to Frue Østergaard for hospitality and, with Dr. Hans Henrik Østergaard, for allowing us access to unpublished material.

Mr. Richard Feachem provided the line drawings and maps and assembled the plates. Mr. Charles Ross Feachem typed the final text.

We should like to acknowledge the great encouragement and help offered by Dr. A. J. N. Prag into whose professional care the subject of this book was first entrusted. We are indebted to Dr. I. M. Stead both for providing information and for inviting us to contribute to the discussions initiated by the British Museum on the matter of The Body in The Bog.

Oliver Caldecott is warmly thanked for his enthusiasm when the book was first proposed, and for help and kindness during its preparation.

THE RIDDLE OF THE BLACKENED BREAD

On Friday, August 1, 1984, a peat cutter in Lindow Moss, near Manchester, found a well-preserved human leg, severed below the knee. The police were called to examine it and supervise the search for further remains: eighteen months previously, part of a human skull had been found nearby. The skull was that of a woman, probably in her thirties or forties, with pronounced brow ridges, but lacking teeth or jaws to aid further identification. Nevertheless, this sparse description fitted a local woman who had vanished mysteriously from her home adjoining Lindow Moss, only a few hundred yards from where the skull was found. The police had always suspected foul play and the discovery of the skull led them to question her husband again. This time he confessed to her murder.

Nothing further was found in the search of Lindow Moss that followed the discovery of the skull, however, and this gave rise to doubts about its identity and age. The extraordinary preservative qualities of peat are well known, and it began to seem possible that the skull was a relic of a much earlier time rather than evidence of a modern murder. Bodies in good states of preservation, dating back more than two thousand years, have been recovered from some European peat bogs, particularly in Denmark in the 1950s. Carbon 14 dating is normally used to decide whether a bog body is a matter for the police or for archaeologists. In keeping with this practice, a portion of the skull was eventually dated at the Harwell Research Laboratories. The result removed almost all possibility that the skull

9

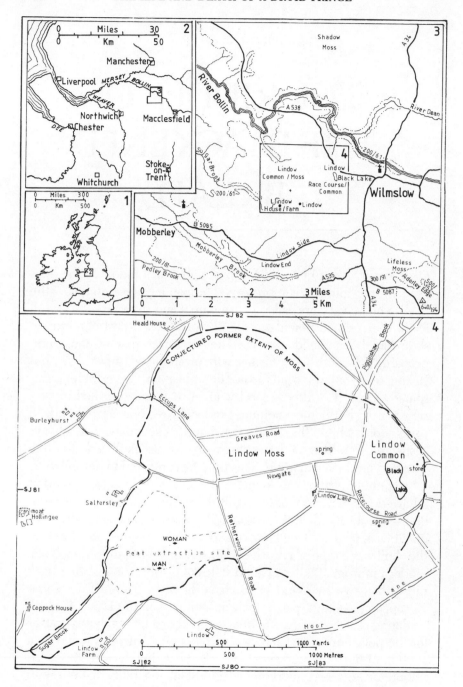

could have belonged to a recent murder victim, because it was at least fifteen hundred years old!

The woman's skull was now classified as an archaeological find and formally named "Lindow Woman," in keeping with the established system of denoting such finds by location and sex. The discovery of the leg, however, raised the possibility that more of the body might yet be found, so the hunt was resumed.

When Rick Turner, the Cheshire County archaeologist, heard about the new discovery, he visited Lindow Moss and inspected the cutting area. It was not long before he spotted a small and blackened flap of skin protruding from the compacted peat in an old work face. This looked as if it might belong to a substantial piece of a body, perhaps as old as the peat layer itself. The skull and the leg had both been discovered after the peat had been extracted by the excavator and deposited for drying. And this delay meant that there was no precise information about depth of burial by the time they were noticed. But the enigmatic flap of skin was a different matter. Its burial depth and undisturbed state were evident at once.

The immediate priority was to remove whatever lay hidden in the compacted peat beyond the flap of skin and treat it to prevent further decay. In principle the task was simple, if arduous: the extent of the body in the peat had to be roughly defined by digging around it and isolating it in a block. This heavy mass would be boxed in with wood, lifted free of the bog, and transported to a laboratory for examination. In any event, the job took several days to organize and complete.

The body, in its mass of peat, was moved to the mortuary of Macclesfield District General Hospital, where it was placed under the jurisdiction of the coroner. Preliminary X-rays of the peat mass and clearing of its upper layers revealed the blurred outlines of a crouching figure. The circumstantial evidence suggested that the body was ancient, but the coroner decided that the final assessment would rest upon an approximate radiocarbon date.

The location of Lindow Moss in west central England. Distinctions between names on the 1842 Ordnance Survey map and modern maps: Lindow Common was Lindow Racecourse; Lindow Moss was Lindow Common; Lindow Farm was Lindow House; the present house named Lindow was absent.

The emerging body and the detached leg were sampled with great care to enable the necessary measurements to be made and to avoid contamination by the surrounding peat. It was vital to avoid such contamination as it would have confused the dating process—the surrounding peat may well have been much older than the body it contained. The initial radiocarbon dating was carried out at Harwell Laboratories where the age of the Lindow Woman skull had been measured.

Rush results pointed clearly to an age greater than a thousand years for both leg and body. The coroner hesitated no longer in handing the body over to the British Museum for scientific examination and preservation.

As the peat was removed, the body of a bearded man was revealed. He was designated Lindow Man by the archaeologists, but nicknamed Pete Marsh by the media, which had eagerly followed every stage of the discovery. Even a thousand-year date made him by far the oldest preserved body found in Britain in modern times. As evidence accumulated, however, he began to look considerably older.

The two most fascinating questions for the archaeologists concerned the manner of his death and the composition of any surviving food in his body. The body's preservation in peat and its great age invited comparisons with the two-thousand-year-old bodies found preserved in Danish peat bogs. In these cases, the cause of death and the last meals recovered from their stomachs had led archaeologists to conclude that these were the bodies of victims used in some sacrifice. Clues showing any relationship between the Danish bog bodies and Lindow Man were eagerly sought.

It was this study of the last meal that brought about our involvement in the investigation. The stomach contents revealed in the autopsy consisted almost exclusively of finely ground cereal grains which, despite severe discoloration by the peat, gave the impression that they had been burned or scorched. Perhaps the last meal was some kind of cereal or bread, hastily prepared and burned in the process? This tentative conclusion was put forward in the BBC television program QED, which featured the discovery, in the spring of 1985. It prompted a chemist, T. Bruce Eve, to write to Dr. Ian Stead, the coordinator of the research program on Lindow Man. Eve pointed out that if the last meal was indeed burned or blackened bread, the occasion was likely to have been a Celtic calendar festival and a sacrificial death. He recalled watching a BBC television program some eight years earlier in which Anne Ross, a Celtic scholar, had described Celtic customs and their survival.

Anne Ross had not seen the *QED* program, although she was aware of the discovery and probable antiquity of the body. One of the most fruitful and important aspects of her work lay in the study of the survival of Celtic customs and beliefs. And this had involved fieldwork in places where Celtic languages survive and also where they had died out but left a legacy of traditions and seasonal festivals. Her research had aroused the interest of the BBC, who had invited her to take part in the *Chronicle* film *The Twilight of the English Celts* which was screened in 1977 and seen by T. Bruce Eve.

Anne Ross's first inkling that there might be a link between the bog body and pagan Celtic religion was prompted by a letter from Ian Stead that pursued Eve's comments. Her instant reaction was that Lindow Man's death was highly significant, and this was underlined by the presence of the burned bread. By this time an autopsy had been performed, and the complex and violent manner of death had become apparent. The body was almost certainly that of a human sacrifice, chosen because the blackened portion of bread had fallen to him. Lindow Man seemed to be the sacrificial victim chosen at some calendar feast and this, in her experience, could only be Beltain, celebrated throughout the pagan world on May 1.

Anne Ross's interest in the bog body was now profoundly aroused. Dr. Stead invited her to write an interpretative chapter for the then forthcoming British Museum publication, *The Body in the Bog*, detailing the evidence upon which her far-reaching and unhesitating conclusion was based. She was then unaware that an even more significant discovery about Lindow Man's last meal was being made by scientists whose specialty was utterly remote from Celtic mythology and folklore. It was a discovery that would substantiate her intuitive conclusion.

The interpretation of Lindow Man's life and death put forward in this book has developed since the publication of our separate work on Lindow Man in *The Body in the Bog*, through which we became aware of each other's work and its significance. For while Anne Ross was developing her initial conclusions about the last meal, Don Robins was engaged with a group of scientific colleagues in a pioneering study of the cereal fragments of the victim's last meal. In this investigation they used a new application of a scientific technique to determine exactly how the meal had been cooked.

This type of research into archaeological food remains had begun some ten years earlier and arose from the discovery of a new application of the arcane technique of electron spin resonance (ESR) to archaeology. ESR enabled us to measure the heat applied to ancient materials and, early on, the team became interested in studying cereal grains. Having refined the method and used it for several interesting projects, we were looking for a fresh challenge at about the time when Lindow Man was discovered.

The archaeobotanists commissioned to analyze the last meal had worked with the ESR team on previous cereal projects. They examined the residues in Lindow Man's gut, and concluded that, unlike the Danish bog victims, he had eaten a carefully burned portion of unleavened barley bread, not a coarse porridge or cereal.

Only when *The Body in the Bog* appeared did we begin to realize the full significance of each other's contributions to the Lindow Man project. The result was the collaboration that eventually produced the far more developed and radical interpretation of Lindow Man's life and death advanced in the present book. It was a chance alliance, resulting from an unexpected intersection between food technology, solid state physics and Celtic ethnography. This interpretation of Lindow Man represents the beginning of a new epoch in our understanding of Britain's Celtic heritage.

CHAPTER ONE

THE SILENT
WITNESS

When finally released from the peat, "Pete Marsh" comprised part of an upper male torso shorn through roughly at the waist, probably in an earlier cutting operation. His remains were squashed and flattened by the pressure of the surrounding peat layers. They were dyed a very dark brown and had almost been turned into leather by the preservative acids and the tanninlike substances in the peat. He lay face down in a slumped position, arms bent under his torso. His left hand was missing and his right only poorly preserved. A squashed and elongated head, which seemed too large for the body, was turned sharply into his right shoulder and tucked in snugly like that of a sleeping bird. A short but full beard and mustache could be seen clearly on the exposed face. This was joined to a full head of short hair plastered against his crown. It was impossible to say whether its ruddy brown color was natural or due to the action of peat acids on the original pigment.

None of these details gave any further clues to the man's antiquity. No clothing was in evidence, except for a band around his upper left arm. This could have meant that he had worn nothing but this band to his death, or had at least been naked to the waist. It was unlikely that the material of his clothing had dissolved in the peat; many fully clothed bodies had been found in peat bogs, the garments sufficiently well preserved to be restored and reconstituted, giving a fascinating glimpse of ancient attire. In Denmark, clothing from as far back as the Bronze Age (more than a thousand years before Christ) had been found in an excellent state of preservation in peaty deposits in many grave mounds. The bog bodies, however, which seemed to have endured a ritual death, were invariably naked or minimally clad. The nakedness of Lindow Man, added to the evidence of the rough radiocarbon age of at least one thousand years and the depth of burial, encouraged the archaeological team in the belief that they had a body at least as old as the Danish ones.

The uncovering of the body made it possible to arrive at a more exact radiocarbon dating. This had to be done, as did most of the other sampling for scientific tests and the all-important autopsy and forensic examination, before the body underwent treatment by the British Museum's conservation staff to arrest further decay. Radiocarbon analysis required samples from several different areas of the body tissues and from fragments of surviving bones. Great care was also necessary to ensure that the samples from the body were not contaminated by the peat, for if this was of a different age from the body a bogus date would be obtained. The peat was to be measured as well; it had been sampled, layer by layer, while the body was being freed and lifted. These samples were not for radiocarbon measurements alone but for a larger-scale mapping of the bog environment at the time of Lindow Man's death with a wide range of botanical and pollen analyses.

Any important ancient object, such as Lindow Man, is never radiocarbon dated by just one laboratory, but by a number of laboratories working independently. This practice ensures that a more accurate result is obtained by treating all the data statistically. In this case, three laboratories—Harwell, Oxford, and the British Museum—shared the samples, both as a check on any problems arising from peat contamination and to avoid error resulting from their different sample preparation and processing routines. While the dating work proceeded, the autopsy and forensic work began, thus preparing the ground for the main analytical program.

THE CELT REVEALED

THE INITIAL radiocarbon results that filtered out from the laboratories were not as clear-cut as the archaeologists would have liked. They all pointed to an age of about two thousand years—roughly the

age of the Danish bog bodies—but the spread was wide: from 300
B.C. to A.D. 500. The results on the peat presented fewer problems,
because they came out consistently at about 300 B.C. This date was
later supported by detailed analysis of the pollen types present. It
was also consistent with current geological understanding of the
formation of the bogs and marshlands between the estuaries of the
rivers Dee and Mersey.

As the radiocarbon dating was refined, however, Lindow Man
emerged as considerably more recent than the formation date of the
peat. The initial dates on the various samples of skin and bone
ranged between a fairly tight cluster about A.D. 50 to 100 at Oxford
to a much wider range, centered close to A.D. 300 at Harwell.
Similar analysis of Lindow Man's stomach contents has recently
been completed at the Oxford Radiocarbon Unit, and published,
and the Director, Dr. Robert Hedges, has kindly told us that the
results also are within the A.D. 50 to 100 range.

Lindow Man, then, was gradually revealed as a contemporary
of the famous Danish bodies that also bore the marks of ritual death.
Such a conclusion confirmed the original archaeological estimate of
his antiquity, but with a substantial bonus. This period of British
antiquity is much better documented and understood than the
equivalent Danish one. And this is because of Britain's contact with
the Romans, starting with Caesar's short-lived invasions in 55 and 54
B.C. At this point, Britain emerged from prehistory and was drawn
increasingly into the orbit of the Roman world. Trading links
developed strongly until the successful Claudian invasion of 43 A.D.,
after which most of Britain was gradually brought within the empire
as a province. Lindow Man's death was placed at the time of the
Roman invasion of Britain. It therefore fits into the early Romano-
British period, which extended from the Claudian invasion until the
early fifth century, when the legions were withdrawn.

Denmark in the first century A.D., on the other hand, was truly
prehistoric. No written culture or direct contact linked it with the
literate classical world, and it is therefore defined archaeologically
rather than historically by the term "Iron Age," denoting the highest
level of technology attained there at that time. Immediately before
the Roman conquest, Britain was also at the end of the prehistoric
Iron Age. The fact that Lindow Man's life and death occurred in a
historical period (or at its very edge) allowed us to draw our first

important inference about him: if he had lived and died at that time and in that place there was every likelihood that he was a *Celt*.

The term "Celt" is often used incorrectly or misleadingly. We talk loosely of the "Celtic fringe" to denote Scotland, Wales, and Ireland. These are regarded as the homelands of the Celts who, it is popularly supposed, were pushed westward by hordes of Angles and Saxons who flooded into the undefended land to forge England by fire and sword after the Romans left. In popular usage, the term "Celtic" is now used less as a political label than as a word denoting artistic and religious characteristics. It conjures up an erroneous picture of short, dark people addicted to magic and the twilight world of mysticism, rather than a specific nationality or nationhood.

As with so many stereotypes, this contains a little truth and many misconceptions. It is often said that history is written by the winners. In this sense the story of the Celts is often distorted because they have been consistently on the losing side for the last two thousand years. Their downfall began when the Romans started their massive drive for empire in the first century B.C. They found the Celts, who had ravaged the Italic peninsula virtually unopposed over the previous two centuries from their tribal lands in south-eastern and central Europe, barring their way. The Romans learned to break the power of the Celtic tribes through developing their formidable legionary system of warfare. Some authors even suggest that the legionary system itself was developed specifically as a desperate Roman response to the Celtic ravaging of the Italic peninsula. However it came about, the unparalleled military force of the Romans led inexorably to the defeat of the Celts and their ultimate downfall.

Under this relentless pressure, the Celts fell back before the Romans in disarray, their rich culture either destroyed or driven underground. It received scant attention from the Roman literati and scholars; few thought fit to comment upon it at all. And it is only recently that the true stature of the Celts and their importance in weaving the fabric of Europe has been fully recognized. The chance survival of Lindow Man's body and the uncovering of his Celtic identity now offers the possibility that a further chapter of this forgotten story may be written.

The starting point for this reappraisal was the autopsy following the uncovering and initial dating of the body, and the expert assessment of how it had been preserved. People were wondering,

The principal cultural regions of Gaul at the time of Julius Caesar.

as they had when every bog body had been found in Denmark, how
Lindow Man could have survived so well through twenty centuries
in the peat. To answer that question we can draw upon a litany of
accidental bodily preservation, and not only in peat.

SURVIVAL AFTER DEATH

MOST CREATURES and plants vanish when they die. Decay and decomposition, and the efficient work of scavengers, combine to scatter their molecules far and wide, leaving no sure trace of previous form or identity. There are a few exceptions to this natural order of things, however, and these chance survivals give us a rare direct view of those who inhabited our past.

Only the slenderest chance preserves ancient bone through the still mysterious processes of fossilization; the likelihood of flesh surviving the ravages of time is even more remote. We can draw an analogy by noting how few buildings survive from even the recent past. Only the merest handful of Saxon and Norman churches, for example, remain in anything approaching their original form. Most surviving Roman buildings in Britain exist only in their foundations or ground plans. As we move further back into antiquity, the survivals that reach our own times grow even fewer, and the form in which they have come to us through the centuries is often dictated by passing fashion and dogma. The great Avebury henge in Wiltshire that we see today was wrecked by the continued efforts of the pious, who associated it with devil worship, and the more pragmatic, who used its stones for house building.

Our picture of the past, drawn from such fragments and chance survivals, is further distorted by the haphazard way they are found and interpreted. Seldom can a discovery be predicted, and in the recent past the true value of ancient survivals has often gone unrecognized, the interpretation distorted by views prevailing at the time. In any history of paleontology we find instances where the true significance of the discovery of ancient dinosaur and mammal bones was crushed in the straitjacket of a cramped biblical time-scale that denied their existence for so long.

Since it is so rare for anything other than a jumble of fossil bones to remain from a creature that died millions of years ago, the chance of error in reconstruction and interpretation is enormous. The exceptional survivals beyond "stone and bone" are fascinating because they are so unusual: a dinosaur's hide or footprints fleetingly captured in soft mud, perhaps, because it hardened fortuitously after contact. In some places, on the margins of ancient lakes, there are even footprint trails of some of the earliest humans.

Oddly enough, one of the earliest discoveries of fossilized footprints was made only a few miles from Lindow Moss. In the soft sand bordering an ancient lagoon, some seventy million years ago, a dinosaur left a curious trail of handlike prints. Victorian geologists uncovered them in the Cheshire sandstone and called the creature Chirotherium ("hand beast").

It is only much nearer our own time that we occasionally find ancient creatures accidentally preserved in the flesh. The most famous examples are the frozen mammoths and woolly rhinoceroses found in Siberian permafrost; one mammoth still had fragments of its last meal between its teeth. Such preservation depends upon the creature dying in an environment that will delay decomposition. The peat bog that preserved Lindow Man is one such. Its effectiveness stems primarily from its exclusion of air, most importantly oxygen; it thereby prevents the onset of oxidation and bacterial decay.

Bodies and objects can often survive for a long time when saturated with water. This sometimes leads to amazing archaeological finds, such as the Tudor man-of-war *Mary Rose* which had been trapped in waterlogged silt. A host of ancient ships, and even very primitive Stone Age craft, owe their survival to the great longevity of certain types of wood when completely immersed in water.

But it is not water alone that has preserved Lindow Man and the other bog bodies so effectively. The peat itself is vitally important as a source of complex natural chemicals similar to tannins, which are normally extracted from bark. These react with the skin proteins and convert them into an enduring and often supple form of leather. While this reaction proceeds, the highly acidic groundwater eats into most of the soft internal organs, fatty deposits and even the bones, weakening and sometimes dissolving them completely. This chemical stew gradually converts the body into a leathery envelope, faithfully capturing the original features, down to wrinkles, fingerprints, beard stubble, fingernails and eyelashes. Often, very little survives inside this leather bag.

Such natural preservation is the opposite of the normal process of decay, in which the flesh rots away from the bones. The bones can, of course, survive for many years before losing their structural integrity and finally crumbling to dust. The effectiveness of peat bog preservation will also depend upon how quickly and deeply the bodies were submerged in the peat or its preservative groundwater and how soon this occurred after death. In many cases, the lightly covered extremities of bodies, such as hands and feet, have decayed more than deeply submerged torsos.

In addition to all these competing reactions of preservation and decomposition there is the physical role of the peat as it accumulates above and around the body, for the organic mass undergoes its own complex formation and decomposition cycles, forcing the body further and further below the newly created surfaces. As this happens, the body is invariably compressed, and even fragmented, so that in some cases it barely resembles a human form when recovered.

A body's survival in recognizable form in compacted peat is never certain, and there is no guarantee that anyone deliberately deposited (or falling accidentally) into a particular bog will be preserved. Survivals in the bogs of western and northern Europe provide a whole range of preservation types. In Scotland, most recovered bodies have been reduced to skeletons, and from the associated clothing, which generally survives very well, none of the bodies seems to be more than a few centuries old. Likewise in Ireland and upland areas of England, most survivals are fragmentary and usually date from the late medieval period onward. Apart from Lindow Man, the fragmentary remains of a second Iron Age body recovered from Lindow Moss—which is still under examination at the time of writing—and the incomplete skull of Lindow Woman are the only human remains of greater antiquity scientifically recorded.

In the peat bogs of Denmark, a large number of Iron Age bodies contemporary with Lindow Man have been found, and a good many are in excellent states of preservation. (We consider these in more detail in Appendix 2 when we note the striking evidence some of these well-preserved bodies present for ritual death.) The Danish bodies coexist with many fragmentary remains of buried bodies, however, and there is no clear-cut evidence that older bodies are either better or worse preserved. Neither does one type of bog seem to be better than another at preserving bodies, for a well-preserved ancient body can often be found close to the very sketchy remains of a modern body in the same bog with the same preservation environment. We have already seen a graphic example of the preservation lottery in Lindow Moss: the virtually boneless leather envelope of Lindow Man existed near the almost fleshless

skull of Lindow Woman, and this despite the bone-dissolving acidity
of the peat water and the more recent date of Lindow Woman.

The macabre case of the moors murders, which took place not
far from Lindow on Saddleworth Moor, north of Manchester, also
highlights the point. Even when they were found within a few years
of burial, very little of the victims' bodies survived other than their
bones. Their clothing, however, showed the resistance to the acid
peat noticed in that recovered from the Bronze Age tombs of
Denmark, and offered the only real hope of identification.

For longevity of accidental bodily preservation in peat, together with the survival of beautiful grave goods, the Mound People
of Denmark are almost unique. Tall and graceful, they were the
rulers of the Danish Bronze Age around 1000 B.C., and were
contemporary with Homeric Greece. They were buried in immense
oaken coffins under conical mounds of earth and were sometimes
preserved only as slimy, proteinaceous outlines by the water
trapped inside the coffins and the tannins naturally extracted by it
from the oak. Extremes of preservation are found even within the
same burial mound. Some bodies remain only as a blur within their
capacious robes, whereas others have been substantially preserved,
with recognizable facial features. And, as always with these chance
survivals, only the ones discovered most recently have been ade-
quately recorded and examined by scientists. Much information on
earlier finds has been lost, either through inadequate preservation,
or through the pillaging and ruin of graves by treasure-seekers.
Some bodies were even reburied in churchyards as presumed
contemporary victims of murder or accident.

The quirk of fate that has preserved people in waterlogged peat
is evident in other environments, notably the climatic extremes of
heat and dryness in deserts and the coldness and dryness of tundra
or high mountains. In the latter instance, the conditions that
brought the almost intact mammoths to us across a gulf of twenty
thousand years have also given us the amazing Pazyryk tombs of the
frozen Altai mountains in southern Siberia, where richly tattooed
warrior chieftains were laid to rest in barbaric splendor more than
two thousand years ago. Not only their bodies but also many of their
tomb furnishings survived in excellent condition, even down to the
coloring of textiles and fur.

Remarkable discoveries of well-preserved bodies dating back
about a thousand years have also been made in the high Andean

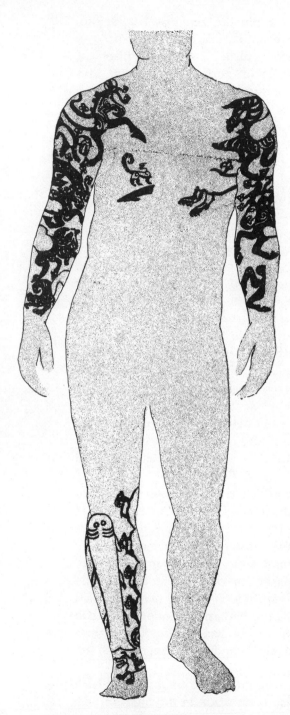

The Celtic practice of painting and tattooing motifs and patterns on people's skin is well attested. Conditions under which skin can be preserved in burial occur very rarely in Europe and the Near East but are found in certain tombs in southern Russia, particularly those which were robbed when the dead were recently buried and were then flooded.

The tattoos illustrated here were found on a body discovered in a tomb of the fifth or sixth century B.C., located at Pazyryk, Altayskaya. The patterns in this case represent stylized creatures and fabulous monsters. The two details shown here occupy the lower part of the right arm, representing a horned mountain ram (left) and a carnivore with gaping jaws (right). A fish and a line of mountain sheep have been preserved on the right leg.

caves of Peru and Chile. Here, rapid and extreme desiccation prevented bacterial decay. A similar mechanism has produced many desiccated survivals of American Indians, dating back hundreds of years, in desert caves in the United States. This rapid desiccation was brought about by intense dry heat. As with the bog bodies, extremes of preservation—from recognizable features and physique on the one hand to a crumbling, fleshless skeleton on the other—can be encountered within one small site, and the reasons for these fluctuations are still a puzzle to archaeological scientists.

A VERY SPECIAL DEATH

As LINDOW MAN emerged from the peat under the painstaking care of the British Museum conservation team, it was not long before the autopsy and X-raying of the body revealed unmistakable signs that his life had ended violently. This brought him closer still to the sacrificial Danish bodies. The analysis started with comprehensive xero-radiography and X-ray scanning sessions which showed up the ghostly remnants of the body's bone structure very clearly.

The distorted and flattened head nestled tightly and obliquely into the right shoulder because of a massive dislocation of the neck vertebrae. Lindow Man's neck was cleanly broken in a manner entirely consistent with death by hanging. His skull was severely fractured at crown and base and his jaw was also broken. Either the fracturing of the skull or the dislocation of the spine at the neck could have killed him, but at this early stage it was impossible to say which had come first, whether they had occurred before or after he had been deposited in the peat, or what had caused them. This would be revealed only if the soft tissues (now turned to leather) surrounding the fractures had survived well enough to surrender their own clues.

The investigators also found that the lower ribs on the right-hand side of the torso, above the lumbar vertebrae sheared off by the excavator, were shattered as if by a heavy blow. The scanning technique was so sensitive that it even picked up slight deformations in the spine which indicated a mild form of arthritis. The fragments of bone remaining in the detached leg, which was now identified beyond doubt as a part of Lindow Man, also gave hints of subtle degeneration due to mild osteoarthritis.

Both findings caused considerable excitement among members of the team who were concerned with studying ancient disease. It was already clear, however, that Lindow Man was not an old or diseased individual who might have been the victim of a mercy killing. The bone shadows appeared to be those of a robust and healthy man; the clear growth of wisdom teeth and the closing of skull sutures likewise pointed to a mature adult male. Even after their first cursory analyses, the pathologists agreed that Lindow Man was well built and muscular, and probably between twenty-five and thirty years of age, thirty years being the choice age of sacrifice.

Detailed examination of the soft tissues started with the wounds on the skull. These soon revealed a clear story of violent injury rather than damage to weakened bones after burial in the peat. The fractures on the crown were accompanied by two adjoining scalp lacerations, each with swollen wound margins, a sure sign that they had been inflicted on a living body. The sharpness of the wound edges indicated that a sharp and heavy weapon such as an axe had been used. Later examination of Lindow Man's mouth showed that his well-preserved molar teeth had been ground together severely enough by the force of the blows for their crowns to be sheared off. He would not have died from these axe strokes at once, but would have lapsed into unconsciousness as a prelude to a slow death. The base of the skull revealed a similar laceration and fracture caused by a blunter but equally heavy weapon, perhaps the reverse or flat of the axe blade.

From this evidence, it seemed possible that Lindow Man had been struck heavily from behind with an axe and then pushed into the peat bog to die. The position of the two closely spaced stunning blows to his crown raised doubts about a simple "ancient mugging" theory of his death, for their angle and severity required the attacker to be directly above and behind him. Lindow Man might have knelt before his attacker and accepted the blows either willingly, or at least without a struggle. Perhaps this had been an execution rather than a ritual death, for none of the ritually killed Danish bodies showed this kind of extensive damage to the head.

The broken jaw displayed no contusion or swelling of the skin at all, this being consistent with the fracturing of weakened bone under the inexorable pressure of the peat thickening above the body as the centuries passed. The blow to the base of the skull could have been delivered when Lindow Man slumped unconscious to the ground after the two terrible blows to the crown.

The evidence for a ritual death, rather than an execution, became stronger with the next stage of the forensic examination. When the torso was turned over from its face-down position, a knotted cord of animal sinew was found around the broken neck. The cord was fitted so tightly that it had sunk deeply into the skin, leaving clear ligature marks on the front and both sides of the neck. There was little doubt about its purpose, for nothing of such simplicity and extreme tightness could conceivably have been an ornament or badge of rank, and the disposition of three knots in the cord was conclusive: it was a garrote. It had been tightened about the neck with literally bone-cracking force and killed Lindow Man cleanly and quickly after the immobilizing blows to the skull.

The principle of a garrote is gruesomely simple. A close-fitting knotted cord is placed about the neck and a stick inserted between it and the surface of the neck. When the stick is rotated, the cord tightens swiftly and with enormous force, first closing the air passages in the neck and then breaking the spinal column. As a killing method it is swift, silent and utterly effective, a combination of hanging (in which the drop breaks the spinal column) and strangulation (in which the air passages are constricted). It was a method of execution and assassination much favored in Sicilian vendettas, and was used as a mercy killing technique by the Spanish Inquisition for those who recanted before they were burned at the stake for their heresy.

Loosening the garrote and exploring the neck region further, the pathologists soon discovered how effective it had been. The air passages were completely closed by the massive constriction. There was little doubt that it was this action that had killed Lindow Man, once he had been rendered unconscious by the axe blows. It thus seemed possible that the stunning had been intended as a merciful release, and this pointed more to ritual death than execution. It also invited comparison with one of the best-known Danish Iron Age bodies, Tollund Man, who had been found with the hanging rope still in place around his neck.

The story of Lindow Man's death did not end there, for in lifting the head to release the garrote the investigators found the first flesh wound that had not been indicated by broken bones during the radiography sessions. Just above the ligature on the hidden right side of the neck there was a peculiar cut in the angle where the head was most steeply tilted in toward the shoulder. At first this was dismissed as a postmortem wound, but further investigation soon revealed its true and horrific nature.

It was a deep and narrow incision, made with a very sharp and pointed blade that had been stabbed into the jugular with surgical precision. From the wound swelling, which was similar to that about the ligature marks, it seemed that this deep and precise stab had occurred when the garroting was still unfinished, for Lindow Man was alive when the cut was made and almost certainly dead before the garroting had finished. The result of this macabre action would have been to empty the body of blood rapidly through the severed jugular. The question of whether this stabbing of the jugular was meant as a killing stroke seemed almost academic, given the rapid finality of the garrote, which had evidently been in knowledgeable and capable hands. Instead, another interpretation could be put on the wound: it was *specifically designed* to empty the body of blood while the garroting was in progress. This was beyond question the hallmark not of execution but of ritual, one still encountered in the slaughter of animals for food in current Jewish and Islamic ritual practice.

Any other wound on Lindow Man had to be an anticlimax after this, and so it proved. The fracturing of part of the rear rib cage seemed to have occurred in life, but a small wound on his chest could have been caused after burial. The final surprise came from the botanists and pollen analysts examining the detailed history of the bog where the body had been found. They came to the conclusion that Lindow Man had been dropped face first into a pool of water about four feet (one meter) deep, rather than into the bog itself, after his complex and gruesome death. In other words, his drowning had been a symbolic rather than an actual end, for it was clear, given his massive injuries, that he was dead before he entered the water. This final piece of evidence pointed overwhelmingly to a ritual death, one far more complex than anything undergone by any of the Danish bodies found so far.

It was a very special death, one that might have been marked by a very special meal before it, if the Danish bodies were anything to go by. So the examination of the internal organs, and the analysis of any traces of surviving food, were awaited with keen interest, not least of all by the authors, for our first direct involvement with Lindow Man began with this next phase of the project.

THE LAST MEAL

THE GRAPHIC DETAIL of Lindow Man's appearance and violent death preserved on his leathery exterior and in the shadowy bones was not matched by the information obtained from his surviving internal organs. Most of them were unrecognizable when the abdominal cavity, so neatly sliced across by the peat cutter, was opened during the autopsy. Careful exploration and examination, however, isolated a tubular structure, which was identified as part of the upper digestive tract. This included the stomach and some of the small intestine, and within these it was possible to discern a small amount of soft, pulpy material. If anything was to be learned about Lindow Man's last meal, it would come from painstaking analysis of this unpromising dark brown sludge.

The main scientific interest in these gut contents centered upon the information they might yield about Iron Age diet and husbandry in relation to the last meals of the Danish bog bodies. It was considered unlikely that residues from dairy products, beverages or meat would survive in the acid environment. Any reconstruction of late Iron Age agricultural scenarios would have to come from plant remains resistant both to the peat acids and to the natural acidity of the gut (the intrinsic acid resistance of the gut had ensured its survival when other internal organs had disappeared). The archaeobotanists have to base their interpretations on surviving roughage—that is, cellulose coatings and fragments, and chance pollen grains trapped in the food remains, both of which can resist acidity.

The preliminary botanical analysis of the ounce or so of sludge from the intestine revealed a finely ground cereal mixture, tentatively identified as bread. This was something of an anticlimax because the last meals of all the ritually killed Danish bog people had been identified as complex mixtures of cereal grain and a huge variety of wild plant seeds—a kind of coarsely ground Iron Age "muesli"—probably eaten as a thick porridge. The complexity of the Danish meals could be interpreted in two ways: either the fields were riddled with weeds and wildflowers and everything had been harvested together, perhaps to bulk out the grain in times of scarcity; or the flower and weed seeds had been added deliberately to the cereal for ritual or religious purposes. Since many of the plants whose seeds were present could easily have grown alongside the cereal, the former view is generally favored among archaeobotanists.

This conclusion about the poor quality of the harvest was strikingly confirmed when Tollund Man's last meal was analyzed in 1954. The Danish archaeologists invited two distinguished English colleagues, Sir Mortimer Wheeler and Professor Glyn Daniel, to eat a cereal made up to the Tollund specification; both pronounced it inedible and unappetizing after a few mouthfuls, even when washed down with fine Danish brandy! There was a strong feeling that the composition of this meal, and other similar ones found later, reflected an agricultural society on the edge of famine rather than one using inefficient agricultural practices, or making a grain and flower blend in honor of a deity. Perhaps the sacrifice of the man, and his consumption of the indigestible meal, was intended to placate the harvest gods and goddesses who had destroyed the crops through waywardness or malice.

The remains of the cereal grain in Lindow Man's gut, recov-

ered as bran and some chaff, was shown to be a well-ground mixture
of some primitive wheat and rye with barley. These were types well
known to the archaeobotanists in the team, and entirely consistent
with the late Iron Age date. Other components were present only in
minute quantities, even in the trapped pollen; some of them,
however, turned out to be very significant.

At first, the simplicity of the recovered meal prompted the
opinion that there was no overt ritual significance in it at all, since it
did not match those of the Danish bodies, Tollund Man and
Grauballe Man. Moreover, the total amount recovered was only
about a tenth of that found in Tollund Man's gut, which had been
recovered intact. There was much speculation about the significance of this observation.

Most of Tollund Man's meal was found in the lower intestine,
which suggested that he had consumed it as a large single serving at
least twelve hours before his death, and that its nutritional value had
been effectively digested during those twelve hours. Lindow Man's
meal differed completely from this, for the recovered bran and chaff
were mixed with some remaining starch crystals, which are rapidly
decomposed in their passage through the upper intestines.

The presence of the starch crystals suggested not only that the
bread had been eaten a short time before death, but also demonstrated a subtle point that had so far escaped comment. The partly
digested grain had only just commenced its long journey through
the digestive tract, and it was quite possible that the small amount
recovered was actually a substantial portion of what had been eaten.
In other words, Lindow Man's last meal, or rather the cereal part
that survived for two thousand years, was only a small portion rather
than the mass of coarse cereal that Tollund Man had consumed.

It was at this point that Don Robins became actively involved in
the Lindow Man project when Gordon Hillman, the senior archae-
obotanist, sought confirmation from Don Robins and his colleagues
that the last meal was indeed bread. This could be established using
the analytical technique known as electron spin resonance (ESR)
to measure the "thermal history" of the chaff and bran—in other
words, by identifying the kind of heating and cooking the cereal had
been subjected to.

ESR had been applied jointly by Don Robins with colleagues in
the Universities of Leicester and London not only to measure these
ancient temperatures but also to determine *how long* the food had

been cooked for. Before that could be done, however, it was essential to carry out lengthy comparison experiments on modern examples of the cereal components to assess the heating regime of the recovered grain. The scientific team had worked with Gordon Hillman before on questions about the heating of ancient cereals, and had accumulated a great deal of experience in handling them. Hillman had obtained their modern counterparts from obscure corners of northeastern Turkey, where peasants still farmed the archaic grain, and from the Butser Hill Iron Age Farm, in Hampshire, where these agricultural relics are cultivated experimentally.

Applying this technique to Lindow Man's last meal confirmed Gordon Hillman's suspicions that the last meal had been a kind of bread. The measured temperature was close to 200° C, far too high for cereal but consistent with baking. The team were able to go further than that, however. They estimated that the heating time had been very short, perhaps only a few minutes, and certainly not the hour or so that might be necessary to cook porridge. Encouraged by this success in framing the thermal history of the last meal so satisfactorily, they began to look at it more closely to see what other information could be gleaned from the unprepossessing sludge that had been so precisely broken down into its bran and chaff fragments.

However, Don Robins was uneasy about deciding so quickly that the cereal grains had in fact been baked in the form of bread. The presence of substantial amounts of barley and the mixture of rye and wheat pointed away from the conventional picture of leavened bread. If the bread had been baked for such a short time at a high temperature and contained such a large amount of barley, it would almost certainly have been in a flat and unleavened form. There would not have been sufficient gluten present to permit significant rising to occur. The original description of the meal as a rather course whole-meal bread, something like a primitive granary loaf, began to seem inadequate.

Wheat, with its critically important gluten, is essential for any rising, and this will occur to some extent even without yeast, because the water in the dough will stretch the gluten as it evaporates. A mixture as heavy as the reconstructed Lindow bread would be unlikely to rise even with yeast present. The gluten network, largely derived from the rye component in this case, would be too tenuous for successful trapping of the gases to occur, especially given the interference from the bran and other roughage components. Thus, the modern equivalent of the last meal would not be coarse whole meal or even pumpernickel rye bread, but something much closer to the traditional Scottish barley biscuit or oatcake. These can only be flat and unleavened, for they are cooked, rather than baked, on a flat hot surface for a short time, almost like a pancake with no appreciable gluten content.

Interest now centered increasingly on the presence of some charcoal-like fragments mixed in with the sludge. The first cursory identification of the dark brown material as cereal roughage had prompted the thought that the meal might have been burned bread (this started Anne Ross's chain of inquiry, which we shall pursue in the next chapter). Gordon Hillman had examined the charcoal-like fragments minutely, and found that they were not carelessly scattered wood charcoal or other fuel from a cooking fire but crushed grains of the pancake or biscuit that had been burned. The ESR analysis added a new dimension to his interpretation by determining that the charred grain had reached a very high temperature, around 400° C, while the heating time had been very short indeed, probably a good deal less than the actual baking of the cake.

It did not look as if the burning had been caused by careless cooking; it seemed rather to be the result of *deliberate* and rapid scorching or searing of a particular part of the cake, possibly after baking. It would appear that the cake could only have been touched quickly with something very hot indeed, almost as if it had been branded.

The small amount of carbonized grain and the overall quantity of partly digested matter found in the gut suddenly pointed to an interesting, though tentative, conclusion: Lindow Man might have consumed only a small marked piece of barley pancake just before his ritual death. And the black mark on the piece might have singled him out for the ritual death the pathologists had uncovered.

The scientific study of Lindow Man's last meal was originally aimed at investigating the agriculture and husbandry of two millennia past. In that it succeeded handsomely. But it also pointed the way into a dark and somber maze of ancient Celtic ritual, which we now enter.

CHAPTER TWO

FACE TO FACE
WITH A DRUID

THE SILENT WITNESS had already provided a mass of evidence through his spectacular injuries and the subtle clues of his last meal. Beyond this, Lindow Man had emerged from the detailed computer reconstruction of his body carried out in the research program as a well-built and heavily muscled man in the prime of life. Apart from minor symptoms of arthritis in leg and spine, which themselves seemed to suggest an active rather than sedentary life-style, and the presence of common parasites in the surviving internal organs, he appeared to be a fine specimen of healthy, well-nourished and physically active manhood, tragically cut down.

Why had such a powerful and active man endured this grisly death? We may say *endured* because of the absence of any signs of struggle or binding on his body, and the clear indication that he had accepted the strokes of the axe upon his crown willingly, or at least without resistance. Why had he been chosen as the victim of this ritual murder? Had his consumption of the burned piece of pancake singled him out? Or had he eaten it to mark his selection by other means, perhaps even through volunteering for death?

To answer these questions we need to explore the significance of many other details of his life and death that came to light in the course of the investigation. Further and more subtle clues, not perceived at first, added to our understanding of the last meal's significance. The last meal was our point of departure into the strange and violent world of Celtic mythology and folklore, the world of Lindow Man.

THE FIRES OF BELENOS

THE FIRST HINTS of burned grain in the last meal had encouraged
Anne Ross to conjecture that it had been consumed at a Beltain
feast. And the establishment of the Celtic date confirmed these
suspicions, as did the unraveling of the recipe for the barley
pancake. This information, combined with botanical evidence that
the death occurred either in winter or in spring, made it possible to
review the case for the Beltain sacrifice of Lindow Man in a new
light.

First, we had to place Beltain within its context as an important
Celtic calendar festival. The Celts used a fourfold division of the year
based on the key points of the agricultural cycle. These turning
points were marked by the four main festivals. Two—Imbolc, on
February 1, and Lughnasa on August 1—took place under the
auspices of a major Celtic deity. Imbolc was the feast of renewal and
purification, sacred to the pagan goddess (and later Christian saint)
Brigit; Lughnasa was the choice festival of the pan-Celtic god Lugos,
otherwise known as Lugh or Lleu. The other two festal times were
Beltain (May 1) under the aegis of the ancient god Belenos; and
Samain (November 1), dedicated to all the gods and denizens of the
Celtic otherworld.

Beltain and Samain were celebrated in periods of great potential danger and uncertainty. Mankind was threatened with failure of
crops and loss of stock at the outset of the unpredictable summer
(Beltain); and with all the dangers of dark, cold and hunger wielded
by hostile powers at the onset of winter (Samain). Fire was an
important element in each of the calendar festivals, but the fires of
Beltain, poised on the threshold of summer, would have had an
urgency and a power that exceeded even the great conflagrations of
Samain.

Most of the great calendar feasts of the Celtic year were later
placed under the protection of the Church. Imbolc was assigned to
St. Brigit; Lughnasa became Lammas, the First Fruits festival;
Samain was changed to All Saints Day, and the solstice feasts of
midsummer and midwinter became St. John's Day and Christmas
respectively. Beltain, however, was assigned no place in the Christian calendar; it was always regarded as a pagan and later as a secular
festival.

Perhaps the most striking and important feature of Beltain was the kindling of massive bonfires, frequently on hilltops. The ancient tradition required lighting two such fires at the festival site to ward off evil and sickness, indeed misfortune of any kind. Livestock were driven between the fires for purification and protection; and sacrificial offerings, both human and animal, were made to the gods who had to be placed at this hazardous time of year. Sometimes animals were committed directly to the blaze as propitiatory offerings.

Descriptions of the great fires of Beltain and the burning of sacrifices call to mind Caesar's famous description of huge wickerwork figures constructed by some of the Gaulish tribes and then filled with living sacrificial victims, both human and animal. These figures were ignited and "the men died in a sea of flame." Caesar may well have been referring to Beltain sacrifices witnessed during his campaigns in Gaul.

The Beltain bonfires were traditionally kindled from *tein-eígin* (need-fire) generated by the friction of a rotating wheel, and this was, perhaps, a link with the wheel-god, Taranis, whom we shall see figuring significantly in Lindow Man's death. It is recorded by Henderson in his *Agricultural Survey of Caithness, 1812* that, as late as 1785, "when one of the stock of any considerable farmer was seized with the murrain, he would send for the charm doctors to superintend the raising of a need-fire." It is in Scotland that the clearest traces of human sacrifice in connection with Beltain have been noted. This evidence is supported by Welsh folklore and there is more than a hint of it in Ireland. In all cases the victim was chosen by means of the burned piece of festival pancake.

THE SACRED PANCAKE

THE CHOICE of the sacrificial victim was allegedly random, although there may well have been occasions when the selection was prearranged. It is not so much the baking of the cake that makes Beltain especially significant, as the attendant rituals. These can be pieced together from customs that survived into the eighteenth and nineteenth centuries, when they were recorded. Thomas Pennant, an antiquarian and scientist, notes several of these in his description of a tour of Scotland made in 1769. He also alludes to a contemporary Gloucestershire custom that reminded him of the Scottish ceremonies he had observed.

Pennant calls the May Day festivities "rural sacrifices" but never refers to an actual sacrifice taking place; there is an implication that his informant requested secrecy on this important point. We have other direct information, however, that fills this gap. It comes from Perthshire, although there are important references from elsewhere in the Celtic world. It must be remembered that such details, recorded by eighteenth- and nineteenth-century antiquarians, were those that survived despite the watchful and vengeful attention of the Church, ever ready to stamp out pagan practices wherever they might be found. The sheer tenacity of these pagan survivals indicates their significance.

It is therefore ironic that we are indebted to James Robertson, Minister of Callander, in Perthshire, for invaluable accounts of the Beltain ceremonies (which were then dying out), given from his unique standpoint as a resident rather than a visiting antiquarian. At the beginning of this century, he told a reporter that the boys in a township or hamlet met on the moors each May 1, kindled a fire, and prepared a meal of eggs and milk resembling custard. Then they kneaded an oatmeal cake that was toasted on a stone among the embers. After the custard had been eaten, they divided the cake into as many similar parts as the number of persons present. They daubed charcoal over one of these until it was perfectly black, and placed all the pieces in a hat. Everyone was blindfolded, and drew out a portion. Whoever drew the black piece was the *devoted* person, and was figuratively sacrificed to Baal. He had to leap three times through the flames.

In Caithness, Pennant noted, the Beltain pancake was probably made from the last sheaf of the previous harvest. Martin Martin, in his *Description of the Western Islands of Scotland* (published in 1719), says that malefactors were burned in the Beltain fire. The *devoted one*—made to leap through the flames, or symbolically thrown on to them—was referred to subsequently as "dead." Caesar said of the fire sacrifices of the Gauls: "They believe the immortal gods delight more in the slaughter of those taken in theft or brigandage or some crime." This ancient May Day custom persisted in the remote, mountainous regions of Perthshire until the First World War.

One of Anne Ross's informants, a native of Perthshire, took her to the site of the sacral square in which the rites described by the Minister James Robertson were performed. She remembered witnessing them as a young girl before the 1914–18 war. The bonfire was lit, an oatmeal pancake was baked, and no matter how much care was taken in the baking of it, a blackened portion *resembling the mark of a huge thumb* appeared. The cake was broken into pieces and placed in a bag, and the onlookers had to draw out a piece, one portion to each person while the pieces lasted. Whoever drew the charred piece was made to leap through the fire, and was then driven from the enclosure with much shouting and demonstration. "He was a kind of scapegoat," the informant said, "but in the old days, he or she would have been sacrificed."

Anne Ross heard a similar story in Derbyshire in 1977, when she saw the Beltain fires lit on May Eve under the pretext of burning farm rubbish. There, only a few miles from where Lindow Man rested, as yet undiscovered in the peat, she was told of the special cake that was baked every Beltain. As in Perthshire, in spite of every care taken, a mysterious blackened area resembling a thumb mark appeared when the baking was complete.

The Beltain festival was concerned not only with prevention but also with fulfillment: with death and sacrifice, and with hope of continuing life and fruition. Side by side with the darker episodes we find happier customs: the garlanded tree or maypole, with its promise of sexual license; the feast on food stored and closely guarded throughout the hazardous months of winter; the promise (perhaps often false) of healthy stock and a rich harvest.

But underlying the tradition of the May Day celebrations were the baking of the ominous bread and the selection of the human sacrifice. These elements were so repugnant to the Church that every effort was made to stamp them out—although the enduring tradition of the hot cross bun may have its roots in an attempt to bring these pagan beliefs into the Christian fold. We might, moreover, ponder on the apocryphal tale of devoutly Christian King Alfred and the burned cakes: the young and desolate king, hiding from the Danes in the marshes of Athelney and being sent forth to snatch victory from the jaws of defeat with the jibes of the old woman whose cakes were allowed to burn ringing in his ears. Did this story echo an ancient and pagan rite conducted somewhere on the remote Somerset marshes?

In linking the burned portion of pancake so closely with Lindow Man's sacrifice, we pose another problem: why was he subjected to such an elaborate death, far beyond the confines of the known Beltain ritual? If his sacrifice was a special event which took place within the Beltain rites, through his identification as the devoted one by the burned pancake, perhaps its importance lay in something to do with the crops. Had there been, for instance, an exceptionally poor harvest, or a succession of poor harvests, which required an exceptional sacrifice?

This idea brings us back to the last meals of the Tollund and Grauballe men. Both had consumed a coarse and inedible cereal full of flower seeds, and this implies that they may have been sacrifices made by a community on the edge of desperate famine. The grain in Lindow Man's pancake bore little resemblance to theirs, for it contained fewer contaminants and was finely ground and of high quality. It certainly gave no evidence of famine, and neither did the powerful physique of the victim.

Careful examination of the gut contents did reveal, though, that very small quantities of charred heather leaves and uncharred leaves and shoots of sphagnum moss were mixed in with the grain. Either the heather had slipped into the last meal accidentally, through its use as a fuel, or it had been introduced deliberately as part of the ceremony. Since the preparation and cooking of the pancake was surrounded by complex rites it seems unlikely that the care spent preparing it would not have extended to the exclusion of stray pieces of fuel. The archaeobotanists had already shown that the charcoal fragments were part of the meal, and the electron spin resonance process had strikingly demonstrated their significance. It seemed likely that the burned heather was part of this ritual as well.

Likewise, it was improbable that the sphagnum moss was a chance contaminant, although it could have been swallowed when Lindow Man's head dropped below the surface of the lake. Forensic examination soon eliminated this possibility completely: the garrote was so tightly bound that nothing could have worked its way down his gullet after it was tightened. The moss must therefore have been consumed well before death as part of a carefully orchestrated and supervised ritual.

The most puzzling contaminants of the last meal were a number of fine animal hairs mixed in with the grain. It has so far proved impossible to identify these. If the grain had been stored (which is certainly likely if the ceremony was at Beltain and drew upon the previous year's crop), contamination by rodents might well be possible, and their hairs could have been inadvertently ground with the grain. If the grain had been reverently and specially stored, however, this seems less likely. Alternatively, the pancake may have been baked (like other festival cakes, such as the Hebridean Struan Micheil cake) upon a ceremonial lambskin, and been contaminated through this contact. In that case, the presence of the hairs might well be deliberate. At present we cannot say definitely whether they were accidental or intended, although we are on safer ground with the most exciting find in Lindow Man's last meal: a few grains of mistletoe pollen.

Since pollen grains are microscopic, it is unlikely that their presence was ever suspected and they were almost certainly not guarded against. The presence of only a few grains of mistletoe pollen suggests that they were a very minor contaminant either in the grain itself or in another component of the last meal that has now vanished, apart from these few grains. If the latter is the case, the pollen is much less likely to have been in a meat or dairy product than a drink of some kind, and this opens up some fascinating possibilities.

Mistletoe has enormous significance in any Celtic context because of its highly sacred character and its association with the Druids. It is a rare plant, which grows as a parasite on lime, apple and hawthorn trees and, rather more commonly, on oak. Its reputation as a medicinal plant is formidable, and even today it is known in Gaelic as "all-heal." Classical authors wrote in great detail about the solemn ceremony which attended the gathering of mistletoe, particularly from oak trees. This gathering was conducted by the Celtic priests or Druids, only at propitious times. The presence of even its pollen grains underlines the ritual significance of mistletoe in the last meal, because at the very least they indicate that the final food, or perhaps drink, was made or stored very close to the sacred plant. Again, it confirms the growing conviction that the ritual of Lindow Man's death was of a very special character.

Perhaps Lindow Man was himself a special person. Was his own status the starting point in his selection as the victim of this complex sacrificial sequence, beginning with the meal and ending in the dark waters of Lindow Moss?

THE HIGHBORN ONE

THE PRIME physical condition of Lindow Man prompted the initial speculation that he was unlikely to have been an Iron Age peasant living on a subsistence diet. However the plainness and smallness of the last meal stood in marked contrast to this theory. Its very austerity seemed to suggest that it was a meal of ritual rather than sustenance. Moreover, as we have seen, the ritual was not rooted in the desperation engendered by failed harvests, as was perhaps the case with the Danish bodies, but in something altogether different. It was part of the awesome Beltain ceremonies heralding the coming of summer.

Lindow Man's fingernails, which were extraordinarily well preserved, confirmed this suspicion. The fingers were not only smooth and unwrinkled—another telltale sign of adequate nutrition—the nails were also beautifully manicured. They were not the scuffed, split nails of a craftsman, laborer, peasant or slave, but those of someone well-born and unacquainted with manual labor. Lindow Man was an aristocrat.

This was another direct link with the Danish bodies. Tollund Man, in particular, had remarkably well-preserved nails which were beautifully manicured. Anyone looking at the preserved head of Tollund Man must be impressed by his calm and decidedly aristocratic expression. Although the squashed features of Lindow Man did not allow any distinct impressions of his demeanor to be gained in the early stages of the investigation, it was immediately evident that they were not distorted by fear or rage. The only clear marks of expression on his face were the extensive furrowed lines on his forehead, which were probably gained well before his death.

Similar evidence for ancient aristocratic status is provided by the chance preservation of a medieval knight buried at St. Bee's Priory in Cumbria. This body was uncovered a decade ago after it was noticed that the coffin was securely wrapped in a layer of lead, which would have ensured bodily survival within. Indeed, the state of bodily preservation was so good that when the chest cavity was incised for autopsy, blood flowed from the wound! The knight had died from an injury that had snapped a rib and driven its jagged edge through his lung. Among many other marvels of preservation, the investigators noted that the fingernails were finely preserved and well manicured. Pursuing this point, Don Brothwell, an archaeologist at London University with a particular interest in ancient diet and disease, carried out some research on the fingernails of living people from a range of occupations. He then compared them with those of the bog bodies, and convincingly linked a good diet and a non-manual occupation with the quality of the nails.

The picture of Lindow Man was growing clearer all the time. The reconstruction of his head and facial features was undertaken by the Manchester University team that had successfully reconstructed Philip of Macedon's features a few years previously. More recently the team helped identify the most badly burned bodies from the 1987 King's Cross Underground fire. Lindow Man, it emerged, possessed a large head with deep-set eyes under a massive bulging brow. From the surviving long bones, his height was estimated at about five feet six inches, and his weight approximately 154 pounds. His O-blood grouping provided further evidence that he was an insular Celt. If that was so, we already knew a great deal more about his aristocratic background than that of his shadowy Danish counterparts, from the writings of classical authors as well as the rich findings of archaeologists over the years.

In the context of our knowledge of the Celtic aristocracy, Lindow Man could most easily be visualized as a swaggering warrior. He would have thundered into battle on his light two-wheeled war-chariot, leaping out with his sharp spear and long sword to engage the enemy while his driver circled behind him. The warrior would either fall or emerge victorious with his trophies of bloody severed heads. Such a man would have been alert to the slightest insult or threat. He would have lived a riotous and ferocious life of endless intertribal battles, usually provoked by the stealing or reclaiming of cattle. He would have listened eagerly to the intricate verses of the bards in the great hall at feast times, waiting to hear his bloody exploits turned into lasting legends that would make his name honored and feared. At his age Lindow Man, as an aristocrat, should have been a skilled and veteran warrior, at the height of his physical prowess and experience, a leader of men.

Such is the picture of Lindow Man as an aristocrat and warrior that we might have constructed from our knowledge of those distant and barbaric times. But when we considered the evidence from the autopsy, there was an enormous gulf between this picture and the reality. How could we reconcile the stereotype of a fierce and proud warrior with the evidence that pointed to Lindow Man's acquiescence in his own death? Was he a prisoner of war, stunned and then subjected to a bloody ritual killing?

It seemed unlikely that he was a noble captive from intertribal wars because he had, literally, kept his head. The Celtic warriors were compulsive headhunters. Their penchant for human sacrifice shocked even the Romans, inured as they were to the horrors and carnage of the amphitheater. Surrender to an enemy never figured largely in the Celtic order of battle. Prisoners of war, as we learn from Julius Caesar, were usually sacrificed to the gods. Caesar reports how captives were burned in giant wicker cages; other writers describe victims hanged on trees as an offering to the gods of battle. The latter was a custom shared with the Teutonic tribes, who sometimes sacrificed all the men in a defeated army, offering the booty of weapons and armor to their gods.

The hanging of Tollund Man has led some commentators to wonder whether he was a member of a vanquished army, but Lindow Man's death was far more complex and savage. So much was done to him that it is unlikely he was sacrificed to just one god after a battle, nor does he seem to have been simply the annual scapegoat at a typical Beltain ceremony. Only one of the Danish bodies comes remotely near the complexity of Lindow Man's death and that is Borremose Man, a close neighbor of Tollund Man. (See Appendix 2.)

It occurred to us, independently at first, that despite the discussion about Lindow Man's aristocratic status, no one had seriously considered what kind of aristocrat he had been. There was an unspoken assumption that he would have led a life of ease, like an eighteenth-century courtier. This unstated view ran totally counter to the violent way of life of the elite Celtic warriors. These were tough men of action, hunting if they were not fighting. They were fond of poetry but, as in the case of the Vikings who followed them, this was a non-literary pursuit geared, in the main, to celebrating and publicizing their prowess and genealogy.

As we looked at the conflicting implications of Lindow Man's aristocratic status, we became convinced that his seeming acceptance of ritual death did not square at all with the role of a veteran and elite fighter. Was there any evidence that supported our growing suspicion that he was *not* a warrior?

There was a clue, subtle and deceptively simple: apart from the

wounds that caused or followed his death, Lindow Man was remarkably *unblemished,* almost like a sacrificial animal from the
pages of the Bible. We wondered how that could be if he had been a
veteran warrior. This question shed new light on the life and death
of Lindow Man. If we looked for evidence that he was a veteran
warrior at the time of his death we found none at all. The starting
point was the concept of the warrior aristocracy as it permeated
European life from the time of Homeric Greece, nearly a thousand
years before Christ, until the end of the medieval period in the
fifteenth century, when its death knell was sounded by the advance
of firearms and gunpowder. The petty but savage wars of this
aristocracy, its muddled codes of honor and barbarous behavior
toward the lower orders characterized European history for some
two and a half millennia.

We have to look beyond the veneer of honor and chivalry, and
even the religion, of the warrior aristocracies to find their fundamental characteristic. This was the lengthy and arduous military
training of their elite fighters. Whatever fighting techniques were
employed, they were all founded upon a long and rigorous training
which commenced when a boy graduated to the company of men
around his seventh or eighth birthday. We have only to consider the
well-known training pattern of medieval chivalry—from page to
squire to armored knight—to appreciate the length of training an
elite Celtic warrior would have undergone.

The enormous value of such lengthy training and experience
was recognized by the Romans, who applied it to their professional
armies with devastating effect, spurred by their experience of the
Celtic invasions. They always put their most battle-hardened and
experienced legionnaires in the rear ranks, to guarantee that the
battle line would never break. The greener troops were kept in
front, and would fight better, knowing that their backs were
protected by very capable soldiers.

The fighting skills of the Celtic warrior aristocracy described by
Julius Caesar in *The Gallic War* must be seen against this backdrop
of intensive and lengthy training, which gave them great individual
prowess in battle. It was the Celtic warbands' lack of concerted
battle tactics that allowed the iron discipline of the Roman legions to
prevail. For Lindow Man to have been one of these elite warriors he
would have endured at least a decade of arduous training and a
further decade of serious intertribal fighting before the time of his

ritual death. He would have accumulated concentrated webs of scar tissue, calluses from armor, even asymmetrical muscular development from the use of weapons in the preferred hand. These specialized muscle actions would have left telltale marks on his surviving bones, for bones can retain remarkably detailed impressions of muscle action on their malleable living surface. Such impressions might have been detected in the highly sensitive scanning that picked up the incipient arthritis, but were nowhere to be seen.

Examination of his surviving tissues, however, provided compelling evidence against warrior status: despite being muscular, physically active and in prime condition, Lindow Man's skin showed no trace of any warlike activity. Either he had miraculously avoided injury or he had never been a warrior at all. His remarkably unblemished appearance gave the eerie impression that he had indeed languished idly, perhaps pampered and well fed from childhood, awaiting the day when his life would be forfeit. But his heavily muscled body, undeniably that of a man of action, refuted this conclusion.

Nothing remotely like Lindow Man had ever been encountered before in all the lurid stories of human sacrifice which had come down from those barbaric times, but then nothing like his complicated death ritual had been met with either. Had Lindow Man really been chosen and groomed for an extraordinary Beltain death? To answer this question we need to return to the sacrifice again and find out why his peculiar death might have placated or invoked the Celts' bloodthirsty gods or goddesses.

THE TRIPLE DEATH

THE CELTS did everything in threes. Three was their sacred number; it linked tales, legends and deities together throughout their society and it is omnipresent in their art and literature. Many of their gods and goddesses have three aspects, and the vast and complex Celtic pantheon is dominated by three mighty gods, each hungry for human sacrifice: Taranis, the thunder god; Esus, the lord and master; and Teutates, the overall god of the people.

Each of these gods was offered his victims in a particular way:

TARANIS the Thunderer, a bronze figurine found at Le Châtelet, on the right bank of the River Marne at Gourzon, midway between St. Dizier and Joinville, Haute-Marne, France.

Taranis required prisoners of war to be burned alive in giant wicker cages, while Esus was offered victims who were either hanged from sacred trees or stabbed to death or both. Teutates, however, took his sacrifices into a watery embrace in the sacred wells and pools that always figured very strongly among Celtic holy sites. These wells and pools were also the receptacles for elaborate and costly offerings of weapons and ornaments to the gods. Our continuing custom of throwing coins into fountains is a distant echo of those powerful pagan rites.

We see individual deaths by stabbing, hanging and drowning among the Danish bog bodies, and stabbing and hanging are by far the most common modes of ritual death. This does not necessarily mean that the Danish bodies suffered death under Celtic ritual, for it is generally supposed that Iron Age Denmark was peopled by Teutonic or Germanic tribes, who had sufficiently bloodthirsty gods of their own. The God Odin, or Woden, who was also the major deity of the pagan Anglo-Saxons and the Scandinavian Vikings, were commonly offered human sacrifices in which victims were hanged from a sacred tree and had their throats slashed. In this way Odin is equated with Esus. Likewise, Taranis with his thunder, lightning and magic hammer has a ready parallel in the Germanic Thor or Thunor. The name of the god Teutates is derived from the Celtic word *teuta*, meaning tribe. He was "god of the tribe" (god of the people). The name "Teuton" is synonymous with "German." A tribe called the Teutones is known to have fought against the Romans in 108 and 105 B.C. The word *Germani* was originally the name of a Celtic tribe which must have been powerful, for a large territory on the right bank of the River Rhine was known as Germania. From this tribal name the word "German" is derived; and the word "Teuton" is synonymous with "German."

At first sight Lindow Man, garroted and with a severed jugular, seemed to be an offering to Esus. Unlike the Tollund and Grauballe men (who were hanged and stabbed, respectively), he suffered both of these death strokes after the initial stunning. But his final resting place in the pool of water appeared to make him an offering to Teutates, the god of the people.

What then of Taranis, the thunderer? If we were looking for a triple offering we had to seek Taranis's share in the opening stages of the ritual, now that we had found the characteristic signs of Esus and Teutates. The fire offering to Taranis clearly resides in the baking of the sacred bread and its ritual searing which was the starting point of the whole ceremony. But important as this eating of the seared slice of pancake was, it seemed to be far outweighed by the offering of the life and blood to Esus and the lifeless body to Teutates. This made us wonder whether the mark of Taranis could be found elsewhere in the ritual. The only place left to look was in the part that we had so far, perhaps unwisely, discounted. This was the stunning of Lindow Man prior to garroting.

Esus felling a tree in which are a bull's head and three cranes, Tarvos Trigaranvs, carved in relief on one side of a four-sided altar stone found in Avgvsta Treverorvm—Trêves or Trier, Luxembourg.

Teutates plunging a human figure into a vat; from one of the inner panels of the Gundestrup caldron, found in Raevemose, near Års, Himmerland, Jutland, Denmark.

We had thought of this as a mercy stroke at first, but as the ceremony began to take shape and the significance of each step was revealed, it seemed less and less likely that any superfluous action would have been included or that the conduct of this very special rite should have been swayed by any considerations of mercy or compassion. The first clue, in looking at the stunning blows, lay in their number, for there were *three*. Two were on the crown and one at the base of the skull. There seemed little doubt that both blows on the crown of the skull had been deliberately and precisely aimed at a stationary target. They had not resulted from a violent attack against a moving victim, where two blows out of a whole onslaught had connected. Likewise, the fracture on the base of the skull also seemed well judged and carefully delivered on a stationary target. And these three blows were from an axe, delivered with the sudden awful force of a thunderbolt, the mark of Taranis.

Truly Lindow Man had died a triple death, through the stunning and lethal blows of the axe, the crushing force of the garrote that choked him and then broke his neck, and the cold embrace of the pool that symbolically drowned him in the final stage. The stab wound to his neck had already been revealed as a precise incision, intended to drain the body of blood, rather than a killing stroke, and we had also noted the significance of the figure three: there were three knots in the sinew cord used in the garroting, just as in the first phase there were three axe blows to his head.

Since each mode of death offered him in turn to a different god, and he probably died at the feast of the mighty Celtic sun god Belenos, the importance of his death went far beyond the initial impression of macabre overkill. Why this special death was visited upon him or why he offered himself for it, as seemed possible, we did not yet know, but already we began to suspect that such an extraordinary death and offering to the gods would not be made on a routine basis, nor with any randomly chosen aristocrat: this special death required a very special person.

If Lindow Man was this special person, *who* was he, and if he was not a warrior, *what* was he? And what was special about him?

A MAN OF SPECIAL GIFTS

THE ENIGMA of Lindow Man grew deeper the further our investigation progressed. We now saw his elaborate death in a startling new perspective, for it placed him on a pinnacle within the Celtic concept of human sacrifice to the gods.

Yet there were still contradictions within his life and death that we had to resolve. On the one hand he had the appearance of an unblemished sacrificial victim and on the other the physique of a powerful man of action who was not a warrior. Unlike a Celtic warrior, he had a full beard rather than the sweeping, tusklike mustaches so evident in Roman depictions of Celtic warriors. And the beard had its own story to tell, for close examination revealed that it had been roughly hacked not long before his death.

If we went back to the earlier premise that there were no idle aristocrats in Celtic times, and we were convinced that Lindow Man was not a warrior, there were two possible careers or occupations that would have been open to him: bard or priest. The bardic life was a peculiarly Celtic phenomenon. Bards were a powerful force in Celtic society, the ultimate repository of a warrior's fame and good name and of the exploits of the tribe and clan. And they were feared, for their clever songs could bring ignominy and ridicule upon any man who crossed them. There was little likelihood that a bard would be killed or sacrificed, because of his great power within the tribe, and the havoc his colleagues would wreak on the reputations of any who dared to strike such a blow. And Lindow Man did not look like a bard. His surviving hand and fingernails provided no evidence for any practice in harping: there were no calluses, no chipping or roughening of the beautiful nails.

We were left, then, with but one choice: he was a pagan priest. Since he was a Celt, that meant one thing. *He was a Druid.*

The Druids were the most mysterious, emotive and intriguing aspect of the whole Celtic system. This shadowy priesthood wielded enormous power, performing bloody sacrifices in sacred groves. Theirs was one of the few religions that Rome proscribed, ostensibly for its blood-lust but in reality because of its political power within the sprawling Celtic kingdoms that later became provinces of the empire. All that was generally known about them was contained in the few disjointed and prejudiced references scattered through the

Bronze figurine, probably representing a Druid, from a deposit
found at Neuvy-en-Sullias, near St.
Benoît-sur-Loire, Loiret, France.

writings of a handful of classical authors, for no archaeological traces of their sanctuaries or shrines have ever been unequivocally identified. Our conclusion that Lindow Man was a Druid drew us into a parallel quest to uncover as much information about them as we could (which we return to in Appendix 1). If Lindow Man really was a Druid, he was the first physical trace of the mysterious cult that had ever been discovered. And we already knew, from our analysis of the last meal, that two druidic associations—with the Beltain festival itself, and the hint of mistletoe—were present. Perhaps the identification of Lindow Man as a Druid would make the magical third connection.

One doubt in our minds about his priestly status centered on his age. The classical writers told of druidic training lasting twenty years, and if we supposed Lindow Man to have been in his late twenties, having started training at seven or eight years of age, he would have just graduated from a druidical school. Why would a fledgling Druid undergo this bloody triple death?

Perhaps the answer lay in taking a different approach to the question. If Lindow Man was special in the tribal or aristocratic sense, and was fitted for sacrifice only when he had also attained the rank of priest, his graduation would have sealed his death warrant. This might have made him doubly special as the object of the triple death. Was there anything that made him *triply* special, or otherwise gave any indication of exalted secular rank?

We had already noted that Lindow Man seemed to have gone naked to his death. His aristocratic status was deduced from his physique and fingernails, his priestly rank from the lack of evidence that he was a warrior. The excessive wrinkling of his forehead might have been a mark of two decades of the rigorous rote learning that, in the absence of a written culture, was a druidic hallmark.

There were no other marks that we could decipher—except one. Lindow Man had not gone completely naked to his death. For around his right arm had been the band that was soon identified as fox fur. Its presence was unlikely to be accidental or casual. It told us something about his status, something very important, if we could decipher its terse and cryptic message. Did it have anything to do with his suspected druidic status?

CHAPTER THREE

LOVERNIOS
REVEALED

SINCE LINDOW MAN was only old enough to be a novitiate Druid, there had to be something else that explained his choice as this special sacrificial victim. We suggest that he was a king or prince, and that the enigmatic fox fur armband indicates his royal status. We believe, too, that the armband is the clue to his *name*. This, we can be sure, held a special significance, for names were not given lightly in the world of the pagan Celts. They had to be earned, or awarded, and were conferred with great ceremony. They signified a great deal about the recipient. To the Celts, a name was sacred, something to be guarded, and withheld when necessary.

Names were conferred on the upper classes, at least, by the Druids. A temporary name was often given at birth, to be replaced by a permanent one thought apposite to an achievement, heroic deed or initiatory rite. Some form of water baptism was used in the naming ceremony, the water being taken, no doubt, from a sacred well, pool or lake, and collected in a holy vessel. Animals and birds played an important part in personal nomenclature, as they did in the whole of Celtic life and religion. The Celts have always evinced a strong feeling for and affinity with animals; it is a fundamental aspect of their culture and their character, for which there is evidence at all stages of their traceable history.

The insular Celts held the dog in particularly high esteem. They incorporated its name into the personal names of many of their gods and heroes. The wolf played a similar role, and is mentioned frequently in heroic and mythological tales.

THE SONS OF THE FOX

THERE IS another doglike creature, however, that is as elusive in the written records of the Celts as is the creature itself in the wild. This is that most elegant and beautiful of our wild mammals, *Vulpes vulpes*, the red fox. But it does occur in early Celtic nomenclature. The early British word is *Lovern*—the Gaulish *Lovernios* or *Lovernos* (Latin *Lovernius*). The word still survives as the common Welsh word for "fox," *llynog*, and the Breton, *louarn*.

Several members of the early Celtic aristocracy are named Lovernios ("fox" or "son of fox"). The most interesting textual reference to a Celtic ruler named Lovernios is made by the Greek writer Athenaeus (late first, early second century A.D.), who recounts a story told by Posidonius, the Stoic philosopher and historian. In an attempt to win popular favor, the Gaulish chieftain Lovernios rode in a chariot over the plains distributing gold and silver to the tens of thousands of Celts who followed him. He made a square enclosure one and a half miles each way, which was filled with vats of expensive liquor. So much food was prepared that for many days all who wished could enjoy the feast, served without a break by the attendants. A poet who arrived too late for the festivities composed a song lauding Lovernios's greatness and lamenting his own tardiness. Lovernios threw a bag of gold to the poet, who ran beside his chariot.

This story, recounted about the beginning of the Christian era, is important for what it tells us about the world in which Lindow Man dwelt. It involves every facet of the pagan Celtic world—a world ruled by the concept of correct behavior, the nice balance of relationships and the "fitness of things." The episode pinpoints the strengths, weaknesses and quirks of the Celtic character.

Since the Lovernios of the story was a powerful aristocrat, possessed of the fabled wealth of the Celtic kings, and held in high esteem, it is clear that the fox was not regarded as a mean predator. To call a man a fox must have implied that his "initiation rites" were somehow connected with foxes; that it was an ancestral name, possibly implying descent from a fox-god or a fox tribe. Or perhaps it meant that he was red-headed, and possessed foxlike intelligence and cunning (and maybe beauty).

The name Lovernios, in the form "Lovernianus," appears

inscribed on a pewter platter, one of a fine set of third-century pewter plates found in 1896 in a gravel quarry at Appleford, Berkshire. The inscription reads, "Lovernianus presented his own purchased acquisitions." These treasures were presumably presented either to a temple, or to a deity direct. The name appears again as "Lovernius" on an altar from the Roman-Celtic temple at Uley, Gloucestershire.

THE FOX OF ULEY

SITUATED ON a height (West Hill) close to the edge of the Cotswold escarpment, the Uley temple site shows signs of religious activity over a long period, and in a variety of cultural circumstances. Close by are a Neolithic long barrow, "Hetty Pegler's Tump," and a Bronze Age round barrow, all of which demonstrate an early superstitious interest in the place. Uley Bury, half a mile to the northwest of Uley, is one of the most impressive hill forts in Gloucester. A gold coin of the Dobunni found in the ditch suggests that this tribe was essentially concerned with the important sanctuary nearby.

The earliest structure revealed on the West Hill site was an oval ditched enclosure; postholes from a wooden building indicated a shrine or temple within. The religious nature of the site was emphasized by three infant burials; a ditch and a votive pit indicated a late Iron Age ritual site. The Uley ritual enclosure has parallels with the sacred enclosures found at Libenice, Czechoslovakia, which also had pits and infant burials, a human skull for libations, and torque-bearing wooden cult-posts. Another, dating to the early Iron Age, at Aulnay-aux-Planches, Marne, France, had five human burials and a series of large postholes, and shows striking similarities to the Uley Iron Age complex. In the second century A.D., two ranges of stone buildings were constructed at Uley, from which coins and pottery have been recovered. They were demolished in the early years of the fourth century. One of them was built over the southeastern part of the Iron Age enclosure; the other resembled the hostelry at the Romano-British temple at Lydney, Gloucestershire.

This complex was constructed during the second century and demolished in the third. There must have been a second- or third-

The Celtic world in the fourth and third centuries B.C.—the La Tène world—as indicated by various discoveries.

century temple here that has not been discovered. A rectangular temple was built in the fourth century on the site. In the center of the building was a large hole for a sacred tree, a "totem pole," or perhaps for a great vat of water or other liquid—blood, mead or ale.

Significantly, the northeastern corner of this late temple was situated directly over the filled-in Iron Age votive pit and ditch, showing striking continuity of sanctity. After A.D. 380, the votive offerings were laid out carefully. Their discovery—including remains of three infants, bronze and other coins, smashed pottery, brooches, figurines and tools, together with more than 250,000 animal bones—testifies to Uley's significance over a long period of time.

The remains of a large cult statue, clearly the insular equivalent of the classical god Mercury, and a bronze of native workmanship of

Mercury as the Celtic knob-horned god, indicate that this was the primary deity to whom the temple was dedicated. Bones from numerous goats, rams and young roosters, creatures sacred to gods of this type, confirm that interpretation. The cock was also sacred to "solar" deities; and a Celtic-type bronze bust of a radiate deity similar to the horned god was also found—a neat conflation of Celtic and Roman cults. Of special interest, in relation to Lindow Man, is an altar decorated with a relief sculpture of Mercury and his cult creatures, the ram and the cock. An inscription on the base tells us that "Lovernius, son of . . . willingly and deservedly paid his vow to Mercury." The name is evidently an aristocratic one. Lovernios of Gaul was a high-ranking nobleman who gave great feasts and scattered gold randomly in return for a praise-poem. Lovernianus used pewter platters and inscribed his name on one of them.

From the second century B.C. to the fifth century A.D., the Celtic word for "fox" is applied to noblemen, and the word from which it is derived is used as a common noun in the British form of Celtic dialects. To find it at Uley, where a powerful god of the Mercury type, Lugos perhaps or Esus, was long-invoked is highly instructive. The pagan temple was replaced by structures that plainly possessed early Christian significance—further proof of the site's ancient sanctity.

Another Lovernius is commemorated on an inscription from Caernarvonshire, dating from the late fifth century. This inscription, reading *Fili Loverni Anatemori,* was found on the lintel of a disused church at Llanfaglan. Further proof of the early use of this name, in Ireland as well as in the Gallic countries, is furnished by the large district in Argyll, Scotland, called Lorne, a name that stems from Irish Loarn, which in turn derives from the older form, Lovernos. This region was named after Loarn, one of the sons of the northern Irish king Erc, who colonized Scotland in the late fifth century.

THE FOX-FUR ARMBAND

WE NOW KNOW Lindow Man was an insular Celt and was a late Iron Age aristocrat. We believe him to have been one of the educated elite of his tribe, probably a druidic priest. He seems to have met his death naked, apart from a band of fox fur about his left forearm. He might possibly have had a cloak of fox fur as well as an armband (cloaks were a status symbol in the insular Celtic world). And this is perhaps indicated by the presence of fur in the peat around the area of the arm where the band lay. The garrote was made from a non-vegetable material; it does not appear to have come from a cow, horse, human, deer, pig or sheep. Could it have been fashioned from fox gut? We know chicken gut was used in the classical world for binding sacrifices.

It seems fairly certain that the natural color of Lindow Man's hair was reddish, fox-colored perhaps. This might account for the presence of the totemic "badge" around his left forearm. He was "of the fox"; he belonged to the fox. We believe his name was *Lovernios*.

In the iron-mining villages near Sheffield, which lies thirty miles to the east of Lindow, there is a tradition of longsword dancing that throws interesting light on Lovernios's sacrifice. The "swords" are actually strips of flat, unsharpened metal about three feet long. There are two teams of longsword dancers, each with six members, at Handsworth and at Grenoside. They perform traditionally on Boxing Day. The "chieftain" of the Grenoside team wears a hat of fox fur, which is an important item in the ritual. The dance is intricate and skilled; it had been passed down from generation to generation in the families of the performers. The culmination is the braiding together of the swords to form the "lock," an intricate pattern which can be varied. At Grenoside, the fox fur hat has the animal's face to the front.

When the men form the "lock," they raise it over the chieftain's head and knock his fox fur hat off as a token execution. As the dance proceeds, the victim is resurrected by the other dancers, as no doubt Lovernios's executioners believed he would be by the deities to whom he was sacrificed. The Grenoside chieftain is decapitated; Lindow Man was garroted. The chieftain wears a cap of fox fur; Lindow Man wore an armband of fur from the same creature.

Sword dancing as a funerary and triumphal rite has a long ancestry among the Celts. The dance is depicted on the back of the funeral couch found in a burial mound at Hochdorf, Baden-Württemberg, which dates to the Hallstatt period beginning about 800 B.C. A triumphant warrior dances on the reverse of a La Tène period coin from Gaul. A version of the savage, virile dance is still performed in the Highlands of Scotland.

Three things are deeply imprinted on the Celtic subconscious: the concept of druidism; the preoccupation with naming, and with ancestors; and a fundamental respect for wild creatures. The majesty and powers of the Druids have always been held in awe. The ritual of naming (among the aristocracy at least), was a druidic function, with its attendant purifying and baptismal ceremonies. Even today in Gaelic-speaking districts of the Scottish Highlands, nicknames (often names of animals and other creatures) are commonplace; and a man can usually trace his ancestry back several generations.

Celtic personal names gave three kinds of information about a man's identity: his *own* name, his *collective* name (the classics stated that the Celts knew themselves by the name of Keltoi, or Celtae), and his *ancestral* name—which would, in the earlier period, have indicated from which pagan god he was descended. Caesar says the Gauls "all assert their descent from Dis Pater and say that it is the druidic belief." Teutates, "god of the people," Cernunnos, "the horned one," Sucellos, "the good striker," the Irish Dagda, "good god," the nameless giant of Cerne Abbas, Dorset: all these and many others seem to fit the description of the father god, the ultimate ancestor of the Celtic tribes.

The third notion that seems rooted in the Celts' thought and religious belief is the fundamental respect that they have always had for wild things—animals, birds, fish, and even plants. Gods, men and tribes are named after them. To say the Celts were animal lovers, to imply that they were unusually compassionate toward animals, would probably be erroneous. But they felt that other creatures coexisted with them, both in this world and in the hereafter, that they had their own powers and, especially, their own magic. It was, Celts believed, possible to learn the languages of the animals and the birds. It was also possible for other creatures to adopt human shapes and vice versa. In the early Celtic world, there were no barriers between things, which all coexisted and mingled in a timeless existence. Death was but an extension of life, and a living creature could appear in any guise without exciting wonder or incredulity. This has been the enduring strength of the Celts in a changing and threatening world. It is the magic that we can discern in the story of Lovernios's acceptance of sacrifice, and his calm descent into the pool which, he knew, was but an entrance into the otherworld of the gods, and of his ancestors.

CHAPTER FOUR

THE FOX'S EARTH

WHY WAS LINDOW MOSS singled out as the setting for Lovernios's final entry into the earth?

We visited Lindow Moss, knowing that we would have to penetrate beyond its present appearance and visualize it in the Celtic landscape of two millennia ago to even approach an answer. At first sight, the area that encompasses Lindow Moss, on the southern fringe of Greater Manchester, is quite unprepossessing and undramatic. It gives no immediate clue to the choice of this place for sacrifice. The remaining Moss occupies only a small area on the western fringe of Wilmslow, close by the perimeter fence of Manchester Airport. Jets whine and growl overhead. At the center of this modern Lindow, however, one comes upon the reason for its ancient name: the Black Lake.

AT THE BLACK LAKE

THE HAMLET of Lindow End, a scattering of unpretentious houses, marks the southern boundary of the old Moss. There is a dramatic view of the heavily wooded flanks of Alderley Edge, a mile beyond Wilmslow to the southeast. Wilmslow, originally a small country town, is now effectively a suburb of Greater Manchester, a pleasant and affluent part of the Manchester stockbroker belt, which stretches out to Alderley Edge and Nether Alderley. Lindow Moss

60

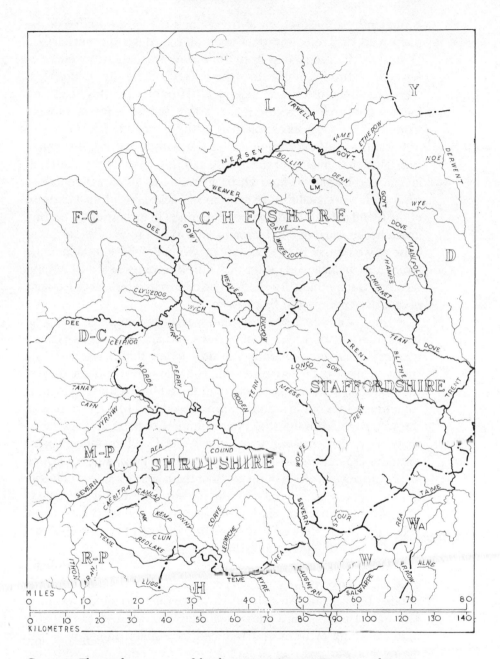

Cornovia. The catchment areas of the three rivers Severn, Weaver, and Trent—
and the three counties Shropshire, Cheshire, and Staffordshire—which together form Cornovia.

is hidden by a thick screen of trees along the western edge of the main road that runs toward Manchester through the outskirts of Wilmslow. It is separated from Wilmslow by the narrow curve of Racecourse Road, a memento of the time when the edge of the Moss was sometimes used as a racetrack. Turning into this road and following its arch of trees one skirts the wooded edge of Lindow Common, the most accessible part of the remaining Moss.

Unlike the larger fragment of the Moss west of Racecourse Road, which is given over to farming and peat cutting, the Common is managed by Macclesfield District Council as an attractive nature reserve. It is designated as a site of special scientific interest because of the blend of heathland and bog contained in its borders. This tiny green haven, surrounded by roads, airport and rows of houses, is as close as we can get to the Lindow of two millennia ago. When one strolls into the neat and rather manicured confines of the Common, it comes as something of a shock to be confronted by a large expanse of sad, dark water—the Black Lake.

Lindow means "black lake" and we had assumed that the name was a relic of the area's Celtic past, perhaps even preserving a memory of Lovernios's end. We now found that it referred to a surviving piece of the environment. The lake—the central feature of the Common—is conserved and maintained by the local council. It sometimes dries out in summer, probably owing to the dropping of the water table through the encroachment of trees and the proximity of ever larger mains drainage systems. Carefully tended paths meander around the lake and crisscross through stretches of birch scrub and open heath. To the north of the lake are patches of boggy ground flecked with bright green mosses. We found clusters of white bog myrtle amid stands of slender reeds and spiky tussocks of yellowing grass. Between them were patches of dark water that gathered into straggling pools.

Wandering between these stretches of mire, it was not difficult to visualize Lovernios's end. There was a sense of isolation amid the rustling birches and dark sheets of water that was almost magical. The din of aircraft and motor vehicles was kept at bay by the protective ring of trees and reduced to a sullen murmur. For a moment it was possible to feel a sense of communion with that savage day nearly two thousand years ago.

The Moss is divided between the parishes of Mobberley and Wilmslow, and had been common land since medieval times.

Freeholders of the two parishes had the right to cut peat for fuel. At that time the Moss extended to some 1,500 acres (600 hectares). Eighteenth- and nineteenth-century records show its accelerating contraction through building and cultivation to 150 acres (300 hectares) by 1843. Today, a mere 125 acres (50 hectares) remain and only a small fraction of this lies in the site of special scientific interest of the Common. The bog had a treacherous reputation in the eighteenth century, when losses of men and cattle by drowning were reported.

The antiquarian W. H. Norbury noted in 1884 that the decomposing skeleton of a boar and a substantial timber causeway had been found in the bog. The boar is a highly significant cult animal in any Celtic context; the causeway could have linked an Iron Age village to firm ground. Norbury also stated that the folk living around the Moss were quite different from surrounding people, with singular physical characteristics and life-styles. Unfortunately, he did not elaborate upon those. But he suggested that the local people were the remnants of an ancient race. Armed with these slender clues, we decided to go further back in time and to start with the formation of the bog itself. Maybe this would shed some light upon Lovernios's mysterious death.

THE COMING OF THE MARSHES

THE ORIGINAL forensic examination of Lindow Man included sampling the surrounding peat, both for radiocarbon dating independent of the body and for the picture its analysis would provide of the ancient landscape at the time of Lindow Man's death. We have already mentioned the latest radiocarbon date of *circa* 300 B.C. for the peat formation, obtained by the British Museum Laboratory, and the laboratory's comment that this predated the deposition of the body. That has been confirmed by the latest redating of the body at the Oxford laboratory.

The reconstruction of the ancient landscape from extracted peat monoliths (long vertical columns cut through the various layers) depends upon both their individual dating and the examination of virtually indestructible pollen grains trapped within them. This study and identification of ancient pollen—palynology—in the hands of an expert can reconstruct ancient vegetation cover in great detail. And the influence of climate and man upon vegetation can often be deduced through the changes marked in the pollen record. Palynology therefore yields a vivid picture of the ancient Moss at the time of Lovernios's death.

The vegetation cover and climate deduced for the Iron Age period, both in Britain and Europe, are intimately linked to the drastic changes that accompanied the introduction of farming from the Near East some eight thousand years ago. There are clear indications that the severe decline in tree cover from that time, deduced from pollen analyses, was caused to a great extent by primitive cultivation. Some archaeobotanists, however, attribute the decline in the broad-leafed tree population shown in the pollen record to climatic factors, which the first farmers then exploited. Whatever interpretation of man's earliest impact on the British environment is finally accepted, the pollen record is unambiguous in depicting the *style* of this earliest British agriculture. It was a "slash-and-burn" technique: small forest clearings were formed by burning and cutting; and they were farmed for a few fruitful years until declining fertility prevented further cultivation. The farmers would then move on to make another clearing while the erstwhile fields returned to the forest.

This primitive form of agriculture calls to mind the Germanic style mentioned by Tacitus. The proto-Celts went through this stage very early, and evolved a highly organized form of agriculture well in advance of their Germanic neighbors. They were also ahead of the civilized south in some respects, for there are several classical references to Gaulish horse-drawn reaping machines—the combine harvesters of their day. Contemporary illustrations of these formidable machines show an inventive skill worthy of a Leonardo da Vinci, and these were practical, working devices rather than hypothetical ones.

From the time of the New Stone Age, some four thousand years before Lovernios died, the pollen record reveals an accelerating rate of clearance of the great British forests. The evidence shows that this change was accompanied by a gradual deterioration of the climate during the two thousand years of the Bronze Age and early Iron Age, until about 400 B.C., when Britain was settled by a recognizably Celtic people. Average temperatures decreased, and rainfall rose. Increasing wetness, together with forest clearance, led

LEFT *Lindow Man's right leg; the first identifiable part to be discovered*

OVERLEAF *Lindow Moss*

ABOVE *Archaeologists at work during the excavation of Lindow Man*

BELOW *Section of Lindow Moss showing the body in its original position, just above the trowel*

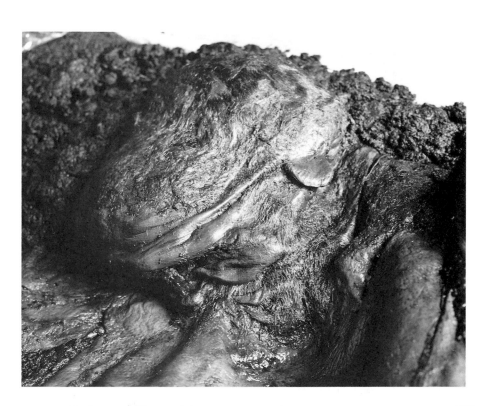

ABOVE *The back of Lindow Man, soon after excavation*

BELOW *The top of Lindow Man's head, showing wounds probably caused by an axe*

TOP LEFT *Lindow Man's head soon after it was freed from the peat, with the top of the ear still folded over*

LEFT *The front of Lindow Man, almost cleaned of peat*

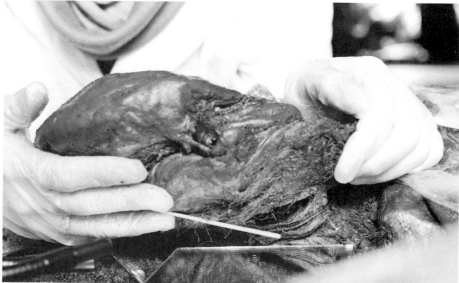

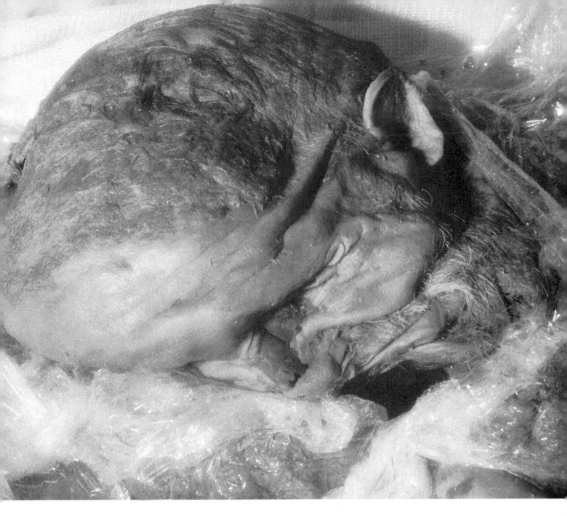

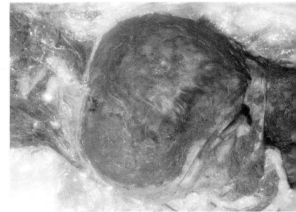

TOP LEFT *The garrotte round Lindow Man's neck with one of the original knots still tied. The well-preserved hair can be clearly seen on the head above the garrotte*

LEFT *The throat of Lindow Man, showing the deep gash which was one of the causes of death*

ABOVE *Infra-red photographs of Lindow Man's head, showing the fracture on the skull and the injury to the crown*

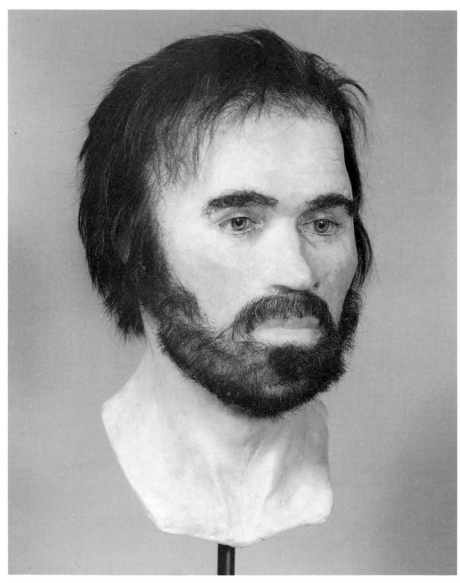

*Reconstruction of Lindow Man's head, partly
based on forensic evidence*

to the formation of extensive marshes and peat bogs, especially around river estuaries. The vast tracts of marshland surrounding the Mersey and Dee estuaries, which bracket the Lindow site, probably date from this time, as do the high moorland bogs to the east. Nevertheless, agriculture seems to have grown steadily through the Bronze Age.

There is, however, a break in this pattern of deteriorating climate and landscape in the pollen record around 400 B.C. Whether this encouraged the development of the more complex social and technological features of the Iron Age is the subject of speculation. The Roman invasions, and the subsequent period of Roman rule up to A.D. 400, seem to have been accompanied by a warming climate which enabled vines to be cultivated in southern England. Caesar reports that the movement of Celtic warbands and armies during his advance from the coast was accompanied by dust clouds, and he describes the disastrous effect of summer storms upon his fleet. Both those facts might indicate hot weather in the middle of the first century B.C. We know that Roman interest in Britain was aroused by the richness of the farmland and the bountiful exports of grain— another pointer to a warm climate at this time.

There is thus little evidence for any catastrophic deterioration of the climate when Lovernios died—by which time, as radiocarbon dating and palynology make clear, Lindow Moss was a well-established and mature bog. Similarly, the Danish ritual deaths and offerings also took place during this period of gradual climatic improvement.

This sunny picture of the late Iron Age has been qualified recently by some fascinating evidence unearthed by researchers who have been combing ancient Chinese records for early astronomical data. The sudden onset of a disastrously cold and wet period in Han dynasty China around the year 205 B.C. had puzzled scholars for many years. It now seems that these terrible years of famine and death (when children were sold openly in markets for food) were linked to a massive volcanic eruption in Iceland dated to 210 B.C. This apparently ejected vast amounts of dust into the atmosphere; Chinese chronicles state that "the stars were lost from view." Detailed studies of Danish bogs have indeed revealed a sudden shadow over the general picture of improving climate during this period, with spells of abnormally wet weather marked in the peat

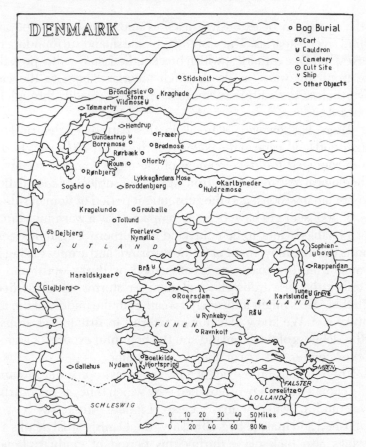

Outline of Denmark showing locations of bog burials and other finds.

column. This aberration has yet to make its presence clearly felt in the British record, however.

We considered the possibility that such a disaster might provide a rationale for a supreme sacrifice. The radiocarbon dates, however, were firmly against this, not only for Lovernios, but also for the Danish bodies. Moreover, the effects of the Icelandic eruption probably lasted for only a few years, and we believed that for a sacrifice as important as that of Lovernios, we must look beyond the possible failure of a few harvests for a single cataclysmic event. Even if one were to accept that a succession of poor harvests required his sacrifice to avert the wrath of the gods, the high quality of the grain components in the last meal would have to be accounted for. The fine grinding, the typical late Iron Age cereal grains, and

the Beltain festival that marked its consumption as the burned slice
of pancake, all pointed to a successful harvest in the previous year.
Whatever triggered Lovernios's death, we could not believe that it
was the fear of impending famine, or a prolonged period of famine in
previous years; his robust and well-nourished physique belied that.

What of the Danish victims? *Their* sacrifices could indeed have
been occasioned by poor harvests; the archaeobotanists' opinion
that the unpalatable cereals that made up their last meals were eaten
in winter or spring suggests that they may have been offerings to the
gods or the earth mother for improved harvests. Nevertheless, the
sacrificial victims do not appear to be suffering from malnutrition
(which can be detected in the remains of some of the "execution"
victims, such as the Winderby Girl) and their radiocarbon dates are

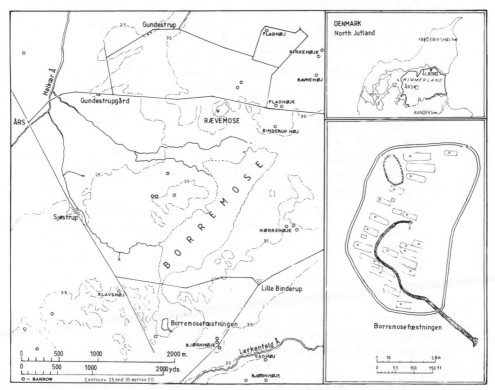

Raevemose and Borremose, Denmark. The former is the place where the
Gundestrup caldron was found, the latter where bog burials have been found
and remains of the Iron Age stronghold survive.

spread throughout the Iron Age. Only one of these—Borremose Man—suffered a triple death that corresponds in any way to Lindow Man (see Appendix 2).

It is possible that a catastrophic event of some kind—which might have been climatic—occurred in the first century B.C. in Britain, because a large number of the great Celtic hillforts were abandoned during this period. They were reoccupied and hurriedly refortified at the time of the Claudian invasion. The cause of such wholesale abandonment remains a puzzle, for many of the southern kingdoms of Britain prospered mightily in this period.

The reason for Lovernios's death, the possible significance of Lindow Moss as the place of death, and any potential link between the two, still eluded us. We decided to examine the folklore and legends of the Lindow area: had Lovernios's death left any mark that could still be deciphered?

THE KING IN THE GROUND

THERE IS a motley collection of stories and legends associated with most peat mosses and bogs. They feature malevolent or mischievous spirits and fairies—variously named "bogans," "boggarts," "bogles" and "bogies"—which inhabit the mire. In northwest England, and also in the Isle of Man, the bogans were terrifying apparitions or spirits, often taking the form of a monstrous ram. In Cheshire and Lancashire the spirits are named "boggarts" or "bugganes," and are said to manifest themselves sometimes as a white cow or horse. At other times they appear as an enormous black dog with glaring, saucerlike eyes, an omen of death. This "monster-in-the-marshes" theme is charged with primitive power, and was drawn upon with enormous effect by Sir Arthur Conan Doyle (a keen student of the arcane and supernatural) in *The Hound of the Baskervilles*. His invocation of the huge phantom dog as the marsh creature drew upon a whole underworld of ghostly and fantastic animals that form a substantial element in British folklore. Many stories may be related to dim recollections of animal totemism dating back to Celtic times and beyond.

This is a factor that we had not considered so far. Our analysis of the symbolism of his fox fur armband did not identify any reason for the sacrifice. We saw the armband as a badge of clan and rank, and a symbol of Lovernios's clan name, the only symbol of secular office and status permitted at the hour of his death. In no way did it seem to point to the occasion which demanded his death. The boggarts were in all likelihood the spirits of people who met an *untimely* death in a bog. Danish bog bodies that suffered execution were all pinioned down with varying degrees of thoroughness, perhaps to restrain their vengeful spirits, which might otherwise arise to seek redress. Such terror of the dead, who might arise to haunt the living unless their spirits were placated, was a feature of many ancient religions.

A more fruitful line of inquiry might lie in studying surviving folk customs that perhaps echo the sacrificial rite. One of the most promising is the Haxey hood game, re-enacted every January 6 (otherwise known as Epiphany or Old Christmas Day). Haxey lies on the borders of Lincolnshire and Humberside, in the Island of Axholme. The village used to be an isolated settlement in a great tract of marshes, and even now retains some of its former remoteness. Several bog bodies were found in these marshes in previous centuries, and antiquarian reports of the discoveries hint that some of them might have suffered a ritual death.

The hood game has attracted a veneer of medieval legend, involving the retrieval of a hood lost by Lady de Mowbray, but there is little doubt that its core is pagan. The ceremony commences at dusk, when the players gather at the center of Haxey village. There are twelve boggans, with a king boggan who carries a long wand of thirteen sticks of willow bound thirteen times as his mark of leadership, and a fool. Standing on the stump of the Old Cross and holding a bran-filled sock tied to the end of a stick by a leather thong, the fool delivers a speech. Toward its end a fire is lit beneath him and his clothing is set afire in the side ceremony of "smoking the fool." Then he leads the assembly to the field where the legendary events associated with Lady de Mowbray's hood—which provide the medieval veneer—are traditionally located.

The king boggan throws twelve hoods (in reality, lengths of thick rope wrapped in leather) into the air. The object of the extremely rough game that follows is for any of the assembly to get the hoods to their respective village inns without being touched by the boggans. But that is not the end of it. One hour after the ceremony has commenced, the king boggan throws into the air the sway hood, the center of the whole ritual, for the main contest. This great length of leather-covered rope is converged upon by gangs from all over the parish and it becomes the center of a ferocious Rugby-type scrimmage, called the "sway." The object is for a gang to get it to its home pub, come what may. That pub then becomes the holder of the hood for the following year. The Haxey hood game is now unique, but several other Fenland villages practiced a version of it until the recent past. The game bears resemblances to other "sacred football matches," such as the Shrove Tuesday games in various parts of the country.

What does the elaborate Haxey game mean? Its links with the marsh spirits, the boggans, seem self-evident. The treatment of the fool (which was even more extreme in earlier times, for he was hung on a rope over smoldering straw and almost asphyxiated before being dropped into the embers) might be a relic of the killing of the sacrificial victim. On the other hand, the mock combat for the hoods does not seem to involve the fool. It has overtones that remind us of one theory of the origin of football: that a sacred and severed head was fought over and the winner kept it as a fertility symbol. The Celts, as we have seen, were headhunters and maintained a deeply rooted cult of the severed head into historical times. Rituals such as the Haxey hood game may be relics of earlier sacred contests or rites.

Despite the hood game's promising antecedents, however, and its link with the marshes, bogs, and fertility cults, we felt that it provided no real clues to the reason for the death of Lovernios. The game is clearly a seasonal event; it is not associated with a ritual meal and does not involve a triple death. If such an ancient seasonal ceremony, carried out in various places throughout the fens and marshes, produced genuine victims every year, and these were deposited in the bogs, we might expect to have come across some of them by now. But none has been found.

We began to explore the folklore of the Lindow area more deeply. The southern edge of Greater Manchester is ringed by lakes or marshes, many of them considerably larger than the Black Lake, but unlike the Black Lake; not all of them are set in marshland. The largest of these lakes is Rostherne Mere, which flows into the River Bollin. This in turn runs around the northern edge of Lindow Moss before emptying into the Mersey.

Rostherne Mere is associated with several curious subterranean legends. One describes how the deep lake communicates with the Irish Sea through a tunnel. Another concerns the Church of St. Mary, which stands on an isolated knoll overlooking the lake. One of the bells fell on to the lakeside when the church tower was being repaired. A laborer exclaimed "Devil take it!," whereupon the bell rolled into the water and could never be recovered. The bell is said to ring faintly from time to time, perhaps rung by the devil or one of his demons. According to another version, a mermaid who lives in the lake sometimes rings it.

More subterranean legends are to be found in Mobberley, near Lindow Moss. A tunnel is supposed to link the old manor house and the church. This type of legend is familiar all over Britain and sometimes has a basis in reality. More interesting is the modern house named Hobcroft Hall in Mobberley, for it owes its name to the reputed haunting of the area by goblins. This echo of subterranean demons comes close to the more familiar boggart legends, and brings them to the very edge of the Lindow Moss where Lovernios lay deep within the ground.

None of these legends dealt with anything specific that we could relate to him. Nevertheless, we felt encouraged, for we now began to see Lovernios in a new light, as a "king in the ground." This idea is immensely powerful. It has its roots in the legends of the *divine victim*, the king who was killed when he passed his prime. (It is an important theme in J. G. Frazer's classic *The Golden Bough*.) The blood of this potent sacrifice and the flesh of his body fertilized the land as the body was crushed into the symbolic embrace of the earth mother. Such beliefs were a vital part of all the agricultural religions, and such sacrifices—or substitutes—became an integral part of ceremonies that greeted the onset of summer, the mysterious season of growth and fruitfulness. One of these, of course, was Beltain, May Eve, the festival of Lovernios's death.

Much has been written about the intricacies and symbolism of May Day festivities, and we shall not repeat the arguments here. We have already mentioned the two key points which bear upon the death of Lovernios: his choice as the *devoted one*, which we established through the reconstruction of the burned slice of barley pancake; and the suspicion that he may also have been a *divine victim*, whose lifeblood slaked the land and whose body was given to the watery embrace of the great god of the people at a time of calamity.

Was Lovernios indeed a "king in the ground," the highest

offering of the people at a time of great trial? Was he a king in his prime, whose physical perfection and priestly status would be kept intact within the embrace of the god until the time of trial was over? Such speculation took us far beyond boggarts, bogans and fools. Instead it confronted us with the fundamental myths of the young sacrificed god—Balder, Tammuz, Adonis, even Christ. For Lovernios truly gave his blood in full measure, and as he entered the pool in the peat, it closed over him like a cave.

To our amazement, we learned that there *was* a legend of a "king in the ground" near Lindow Moss. Alderley Edge, that whalebacked ridge that we saw hanging over Lindow Moss as we approached Wilmslow, is the scene of a peculiar and powerful legend that now assumed a new significance for us. The legend concerns King Arthur and a magician with some very druidic characteristics. In its simplest form the legend is stated thus:

A farmer was going to Macclesfield market with a beautiful white mare. As he passed Alderley Edge he was approached by a wizard who offered him a very good price for it. The farmer refused, saying that he would sell it for more in the market. However, although many people showed great interest in the horse, no one at the market offered him the price he wanted, so he went back home with the horse. The wizard was waiting for him again, and this time the farmer accepted his offer and pocketed the money. The wizard asked him to lead the horse down through the woods to a rock. When he touched the rock a great gate appeared and opened. The wizard told the farmer that King Arthur and his knights were sleeping there until they were needed by England once again, and that one knight lacked a horse. Seeing the truth of the wizard's words, the farmer fled with his money.

Legends of sleeping kings and heroes, who will awaken in their country's hour of need, occur in many parts of the British Isles and Europe. They cluster around the name of Arthur, and they are even linked to Drake in Devon. They are not so common, however, that the coincidence between the proximity of this legendary site and Lindow can be dismissed out of hand. Alderley Edge has caves and also mines; it was exploited in Roman times, and probably earlier, for copper. Whether it played any role in the sacrifice of Lindow Man is a question we address later. First we had to determine whether there was some ancient memory of a "king in the ground," which was later transferred to Arthur while keeping its druidic overtones in the shape of the wizard. A possible clue lies in the commemoration of this legend at a wishing well on the Edge which has strong Celtic connections. Another is in the figure of the white horse, a specially sacred Celtic animal. The root of its Celtic name, *mandua,* "pony," occurs in the name of the powerful queen of the Brigantes, Cartimandua, "sleek pony," who comes into the story on page 85.

There are more tangible links to a rite associated with horses and divine victims in the area, however, for at Ashton-under-Lyme the peculiar ceremony of "riding the black lad," held every Easter Monday until the 1960s, casts a strange light upon the Lindow sacrifice. The effigy of a knight in black armor and cloak was mounted on a horse and paraded through the town. Finally, it was set up as a target, to be pelted with refuse and stones, while everyone jeered at it. This custom has a medieval veneer, for it is linked to the execration of a harsh knight landlord from the fifteenth century, but the ancient "scapegoat" character is too clear to be ignored. We found in this legend an unmistakable echo of an aristocrat being loaded with the people's misfortunes and then ritually killed as the divine victim.

Another example of this peculiar Easter Monday custom survived until the last century at nearby Neston. It was called "riding the lord." A man rode a donkey through the village while the inhabitants threw rubbish at him. We felt that the concentration of such legends and tales in the area might provide a hint of the singular event of two thousand years ago that we were looking for. Perhaps Lovernios had suffered some formal execration as the scapegoat, just as the Beltain victims did in living memory. It would fit in well with his choice as the *devoted one.*

The horse that carries the victim figures in another unique Cheshire folk survival, the Wild Horse of Antrobus. The Antrobus mummers' play provides its vehicle; like many such old plays, it deals with the death and resurrection of the hero. In this case he is the Black Prince of Paradise. The play is the only recorded mummers' play that involves a horse.

Our survey of the scattered folklore evidence, although inevitably full of intangibles, pointed toward a cluster of legends that might be an echo of a scapegoat king: the involvement of a horse, the sleeping of the king underground, the fox fur symbol, and death and rebirth of the divine victim. The convergence of the three strands of evidence for *divine victim, devoted one* and the Beltain sacrifice underlined the *Celtic* significance of the sacrifice. If this was indeed a dim shadow of Lovernios's sacrifice, perhaps we would obtain a sharper image by turning to the Celtic aspects of the region in more detail. It was this investigation that finally began to uncover the significance of Lindow Moss.

THE TRIPLE BOUNDARY

LINDOW MOSS lies in a shallow, saucer-shaped depression bounded on the northern edge by the River Bollin, which flows down from the Pennines into the Mersey. This great river, as shown by the Old English derivation of its name Maeres-ea, literally means "boundary river." It probably derives from its function as a frontier between the Anglo-Saxon kingdom of Mercia and the unconquered British of Cumbria, whom the Welsh knew as the "men of the north."

Cheshire itself was originally part of Mercia, but did not become a distinct shire until the tenth century. Chester was first mentioned—as Leageceaster, the City of the Legion—in the *Anglo-Saxon Chronicle* for the year 979. At that time Lancashire did not yet exist; the land north of Chester was still hostile British territory. It was called the land of the Pecsaetan, a clear indication that the original Celtic inhabitants, a tribe of the ancient Brigantian confederacy called the Setantii, still lived there. This tribal name also embodied the Latin name of the Mersey: Seteia flumen. The Setantii were far from being an obscure Celtic tribe locked behind the marshes during the English advance. They had won enduring fame through giving the Irish of Ulster their legendary hero Cú Chulainn.

The fact that the Anglo-Saxons recognized this area as a strong Celtic enclave underlies the importance of the Celtic myths that surround it and which involve Lindow, just across the Mersey. South of the Boundary River there was also a strong Celtic presence in the nearby Wirral peninsula. The farthest tip of the peninsula, Wallasey, means "the island of Welshmen." The Celtic presence, persisting well into Anglo-Saxon times, is underlined by a name given to the inhabitants of Wirral by the Saxons—the Kilguri. This is a rendering of another Celtic tribe, the Cornovii, who gave their

name to the Celtic kingdom of Cornovia. Lindow Moss is in
Cornovia.

The Mersey, in Celtic times, formed a tribal boundary around
the Cornovii, dividing them from the Brigantian confederacy to the
north. Cornovian territory probably comprised, approximately,
modern Cheshire, Shropshire and Staffordshire. Like most Celtic
kingdoms, it is best defined not by the later Saxon shires and
counties but by river boundaries.

The catchment area of the three great rivers—Upper Severn,
Weaver and Upper Trent—defined the main territory of Cornovia.
The Mersey, with its extensive marshlands, was the natural northern boundary. The eastern frontier was formed by an arc of connecting rivers—Goyt, Dove, Trent and Tame. The southern frontier probably followed the line of the Teme and the Salwarpe. On
the west, the boundary would have followed the headwaters of the
Teme and part of the line of the Dee over the foothills of the
Cambrian Mountains.

To the east of the Cornovii were the lands of the Corieltavi, and
to the west the Decangli. Lindow Moss, five miles from the Mersey
and eight from the Goyt, lay in the northeastern corner of Cornovia,
close to where its border abutted those of Brigantia and Corieltavia.

It is tempting to see Lindow as a special place, where the
boundaries of these three Celtic kingdoms met. To do so, however,
overstates the case. For the boundaries that we have sketched are
not those of autonomous states or kingdoms, but loose tribal
groupings with far less political cohesion than those in the southeast.
There, trading links with Roman Europe brought Celtic society into
the mainstream of classical culture.

Although the rivers probably formed substantive boundaries
between these tribal groupings, we may imagine that there were
constant raids and intertribal disputes across them. The idea of the
Mersey forming a natural frontier, with Lindow tucked securely
behind its confluence with the Goyt and the barrier of the marshes,
is borne out by later historical events in the area.

Chester, which began life as Deva, a strategically situated
legionary encampment in the Dee estuary, remained an important
strategic center in northwest England until the reign of Richard II,
when progressive silting of the Dee curtailed its maritime role. The
Wirral peninsula continued to provide military port facilities well
past the medieval period, and it was an important embarkation point

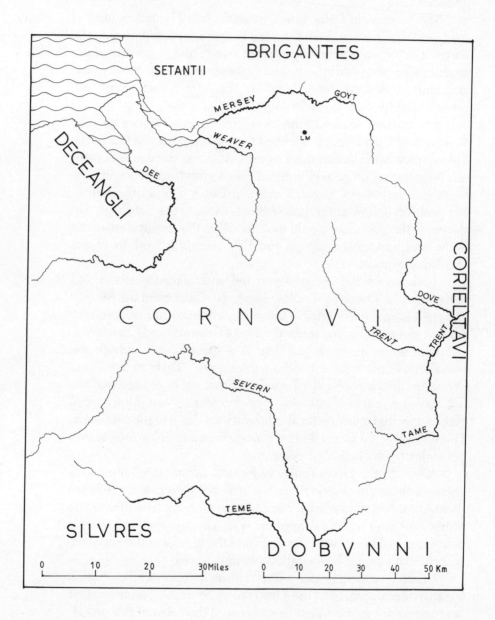

The Cornovii and their British neighbors.

for Ireland until after the time of Cromwell. In Anglo-Saxon times, the area played a vital role in the wars with the Danes. Several authorities maintain that the critical tenth-century battle of Brunanburgh—which brought the Viking armies to a halt—was fought near Chester. The Roman conquest of Wales and northern England under Agricola was based on Chester, which was only eclipsed in importance when York (Eboracum) was fortified. Chester remained one of the three great legionary fortresses of Roman Britain and the present city has many fine Roman remains.

The strategic importance of this corner of northwest Britain obviously declined after the pacification of Wales and Scotland. Centuries later, however, the seeds of the Industrial Revolution took root there. The development of the vast northwestern industrial conurbation is a story that goes far beyond our scope, but it has occurred to us that there must be an underlying reason why the area assumed such a pivotal role in the growth of Britain. We say *Britain,* because the part played by the northwest in English history has to be seen against the background of a stubborn and enduring Celtic presence in the area. The antiquarian's comments on the singularity of the population around Lindow provided one indication of that. Modern Lancashire is sandwiched between Celtic Wales and Cumbria, the home of the Welshmen's cousins, Gwyry Goyledd, the "Men of the North," which retains many of its Celtic links. To its west is the Celtic Isle of Man and the *insula sacra* of Ireland. And to the east are the most intriguing survivals of all.

CELTIC SURVIVALS

THE ENDURING Beltain fires, and customs of the High Peak in Derbyshire have already been mentioned. Further evidence for the strong continuity of Celtic customs in this remote part of England is provided by the widespread Derbyshire "well dressing" ceremonies. These ceremonies are Christianized relics of ancient pagan Celtic well-worship, which was often subsumed under the protection of Christian saints. Other Celtic survivals are just as strong. Perhaps the most striking is the persistence of the stone head cult. There is considerable evidence that these heads continue to be carved in the Celtic style, and none of it points to any attempt to produce counterfeit heads. It is a living tradition that persists despite the leveling effect of twentieth-century culture.

Significant Celtic customs survive in the folk memory to hint at the role of human sacrifice in the former Celtic religion of the region. We could add to this our newly won perception of the pivotal role of this region in British history, and ask whether the strong Celtic presence has helped to determine this role. Or perhaps we should have framed the question differently: did the historical significance of the region give any clue to its significance as the site of Lovernios's death?

Was it the choice of Lindow for this complex and unique sacrificial death that attracted the dense cluster of Celtic influences in this land between the rivers? Did the triple boundary mark not the conjunction of Celtic kingdoms, but a Celtic enclave, with Lindow at its center?

CHAPTER FIVE

THE BLACK YEAR

THE DEATH of Lovernios was too elaborate for a routine sacrifice. It was a very special event: special in that it was a triple death brought about at the feast of Belenos, and special in the choice of the high-born and priestly Lovernios as the willing victim. These striking features pointed to a powerful motive and to a significance in Lindow Moss that we had not yet uncovered. Such a sacrifice, we felt, would have been offered neither annually nor routinely. It had to be a unique event triggered by unique circumstances, and we could only suppose that the event was a sudden catastrophe. Our quest for the meaning of the life and death of Lovernios, the druid prince, now led us inexorably to the uncovering of the catastrophe.

What kind of event could have triggered such a powerful symbolic response, which worked its way into local folklore, leaving echoes of the archetypal myths of the young god dying and being resurrected? Only an apocalyptic disaster of the first magnitude would have called forth this unprecedented and unparalleled sacrifice.

In the previous chapter we considered the short period of worsening climate, starting around 210 B.C., which transformed farmland and forest into bogs and marshes. This, however, though it might have had a bearing upon the Danish sacrifices, was too early to have provoked that of Lovernios. The confirmed radiocarbon date placed his death firmly in the second half of the first century A.D. This period was dominated by one catastrophic fact: the Roman conquest of Britain. How did that conquest affect the area around

79

Celtic tribal names in Britain and Ireland, with the sites of Lindow Moss, Llyn Cerrig Bach, and place names incorporating *nemet-*, meaning "grove" or "sanctuary."

Lindow Moss? And how could it have led to the supreme sacrifice? To answer these questions we had to chart the progress of the conquest until it engulfed the land of the Cornovii.

UNDER THE ROMAN HEEL

THE CLAUDIAN INVASION of A.D. 43 had dire consequences for Celtic Britain. It was the third Roman invasion of Britain, following Julius Caesar's two previous attempts in 55 and 54 B.C., neither of which were sustained attempts at conquest. It came when the memory of Caesar's attacks had faded and when the British Celts may have doubted whether Rome would ever try for outright conquest again.

The third invasion, led by Aulus Plautius, differed from Caesar's abortive attempts in one very significant way. The landing, at Richborough, in Kent, was unopposed by the Celts. Plautius and his army finally faced a united tribal army under Caratacus at the crossing of the River Medway, but Caratacus was routed and sent fleeing westward. Plautius regrouped carefully after the battle, and awaited the arrival of reinforcements led by Emperor Claudius himself.

The combined army moved on and, Tacitus reports, won another battle at Brentwood, after which it secured the surrender of eleven British kings in the southeast. Moving northward, it took the Belgic stronghold at what is now Colchester. The city of Camulodunum was founded there as the nucleus of the new province of Britannia. The southeastern kingdoms had become semi-Romanized through increasing trading contacts with the Roman world since Caesar's abortive raids, and they soon came fully within the Roman fold. The kingdom of the Atrebates, centered upon Silchester, near Reading, and covering much of modern Hampshire, was already a client state of the Romans. With Colchester as a secure base, Plautius established the first frontier of the fledgling Roman province along the line of the Fosse Way, which still connects modern Lincoln with Leicester, Cirencester and Bath. This frontier was the beginning of the Roman road system, which was to link forts and towns as the province gradually took shape. Plautius pushed steadily northward into Lincolnshire and sent

Vespasian deep into the southwest, where he carried all before him.

It is possible that the prospect of an even more luxurious life-style meant that the southern Belgic nobles accepted the Roman invasion without too much difficulty. There was, however, plenty of fight left elsewhere. Caratacus had taken refuge among the warlike Silures and Ordovices, whose kingdoms were in the remote hills and valleys of south and central Wales. Beyond them lay the tribal confederacy of the Brigantes, spread across a large tract of England north of the Mersey. They were as yet unfought by the Romans, but not untouched by Roman diplomacy: the confederacy was riven by deep divisions which the Romans were already exploiting. Further north and west was unknown, unmapped and hostile territory. The Roman province based upon Colchester and the southeastern kingdoms was not necessarily set to grow swiftly or even to endure. Caesar had withdrawn; maybe Claudius would do so as well. Caratacus and his men might have reasoned thus, to encourage themselves in their dour guerrilla war in the mountains.

The invasion of A.D. 43 cannot be seen as an irrevocable disaster in itself. The possibility of a British revival (centered upon Caratacus's base among the Silures and Ordovices), and the even-tual defeat of the Romans could not be dismissed. And the Romans might at any time decide to pull back to the natural frontier of the Gaulish coast if resistance stiffened. They had withdrawn to the Rhine after their abortive German adventures only a few decades before, and they might adopt a similar strategy now. Encouraging as such thoughts may have been to the Britons, however, there was a striking difference between the time of Caesar and that of Claudius that made such a development unlikely. Rome was no longer a republic. It was now an empire under the command of one man, its armies marching at the whim of that man, who was also a god. Where Rome now went, the worship of the emperor went, too. And if the emperor decreed that a country should be conquered, the legions would march. Caligula had tried to launch an invasion of Britain in a capricious moment. But Claudius was in earnest, and the four legions now on British soil looked set to stay at his command.

Emperor worship by itself need not have caused great diffi-culties among the Celts, but the Roman antipathy toward the Celtic priesthood was another matter altogether. Caesar had not stayed long enough to consider or take any action against the British

Druids, and the account of the Druids in his *Gallic War* is not unsympathetic. But from the time of Augustus, the first emperor, Roman hostility toward the Druids in the newly won province of Gaul had mounted. What then of the Druids in Britain, and of the sacrificed Druid—Lovernios?

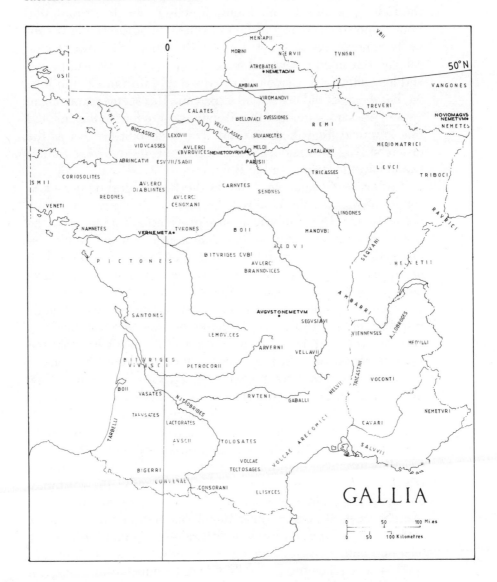

Celtic tribal names in Gaul, with place names incorporating *nemet-*, meaning "grove" or "sanctuary."

THE CAMPAIGN AGAINST THE DRUIDS

BOTH AUGUSTUS and his successor Tiberius published edicts against the Celtic priesthood. The ostensible reasons for the proscription hinged upon the barbarity of their sacrifices, but the real motives are likely to have been political. Despite the edicts, the pagan Celtic religion remained a powerful force throughout the Roman period and long afterward. Claudius proscribed druidism in Gaul in A.D. 54, but the edict did not extend to Britain. This seems surprising in view of Caesar's statement that Britain was the font of the cult and that it spread from there to Gaul. The probability is that as the orders of Augustus and Tiberius were applied, surviving Druids would have fled from Gaul to Britain.

After the Claudian invasion, as the Roman grip tightened on southern England, the Druids would have melted away to a more distant refuge. The focus of resistance provided by Caratacus among the Silures and Ordovices of the Cambrian mountains would undoubtedly have attracted them and they may have helped to organize it. If that is the case, their base would almost certainly have been Mona, the sacred Island of Anglesey, the haven and granary of Caratacus's struggle. This renewed resistance drew a sharp Roman response, judging by the assault on the southwestern forts that may have harbored the Druids. And there is little to suggest that the Romans would have had any difficulty in subduing the remote mountain strongholds of the Silures and Ordovices when they moved against them in earnest.

The ferocious and bloody campaigns in Dorset and North Wales, if they were launched against druidic power bases, might account for the fact that the Druids in Britain were not proscribed. Claudius may have determined that they should simply be put to the sword. But whatever happened to the Druids, the worship of the Celtic gods continued unabated. There is an enormous amount of archaeological evidence that Roman pantheism was integrated with the native religion throughout Britain, and that the Romans tolerated and even worshiped British gods. The same is true of Gaul. This typifies the generally tolerant Roman attitude toward alien religions, however bizarre, that did not conflict with emperor worship. There must have been other motives for the implacable

Roman pursuit of the Druids, and the destruction of their pan-tribal role.

Can we discern the hands of the Druids behind the continuing battles between Celts and Romans? The Silures launched repeated attacks into the new province during the years immediately after the invasion. The governor, Ostorius Scapula, counterattacked vigorously and harried them through the central Welsh mountains in a series of campaigns starting in A.D. 47. Caratacus again confronted the Romans in a battle near Snowdon; once more he was decisively beaten. This time he fled northward into Brigantia, but there his luck deserted him. The Brigantian Queen, Cartimandua, who was friendly toward the Romans, handed him over in chains. Even without Caratacus the Silures fought on, but no further serious

Bronze figurine, probably a British priest licensed to practice Romanized Celtic cults, found in a gravel pit at Earith, Cambridgeshire, England, in 1978.

attempts were made to subdue them, until A.D. 58. In that year a new governor, Suetonius Paulinus, was appointed by Nero, who had succeeded to the imperial throne on the death of Claudius in A.D. 54. In the fifteen years between the invasion and the arrival of Suetonius, the Roman grip on the island had tightened. Land near Colchester was taken for retired legionnaires to settle on, and the carrying of arms by the native Celts was banned. The resulting ill-feeling spilled over into a short-lived revolt among the Iceni, whose kingdom covered modern Norfolk.

The appointment of Suetonius heralded a tough new approach to the settlement of Britain—and the campaign against the Druids. Nero had espoused complete absolutism in Rome. This, and his profligacy with imperial revenues, encouraged him to look around the empire for more funds to replenish the depleted treasury. His gaze soon lit upon Britain, whose wealth had not so far resulted in the expected flow of revenues. This was due in large part to the Silures and Ordovices, who denied access to the lead and copper deposits in the Welsh mountains, keeping the legions occupied in troublesome and expensive guerrilla warfare. Suetonius was appointed specifically to defeat the Silures and Ordovices. To accomplish that, he had to destroy not only their armies and warbands but also their supply lines and their base in Anglesey. This island was the granary of the resistance and the ultimate druidic stronghold. With one well-organized campaign, therefore, the Romans could eliminate the armed threat to the new province by circling around the mountains and smashing both the stronghold of resistance and the Druids. They identified Anglesey as the key to their campaign.

Suetonius was an ideal choice for this task. He had just concluded a brilliantly successful campaign against the Moors in Mauritania, where the military problems—guerrilla warfare in the mountains supplied by bases beyond—were strikingly similar to those that faced him in Wales. He approached his new task single-mindedly, one eye undoubtedly upon a second triumph in Rome. The religious proscription seems to have concerned him less than the military threat. Or he may have considered them to be different sides of the same coin. The key to his strategy, in any case, was the elimination of the supply base—material and spiritual—in Anglesey. That meant the physical destruction of the Druids and their most important sanctuary.

The marshaling of his forces for the attack on Mona and the

encirclement of the mountain fastness of Snowdonia brought the Roman forces close to Lindow Moss early in A.D. 60. Then came three great disasters which made that year the blackest that Celtic Britain was ever to endure. Uncovering the full significance of the black year gave us the key. It explained, in a quite unexpected way, why Lindow Moss had been chosen for the supreme sacrifice of Lovernios.

THE BLACK SPRING

SUETONIUS'S ARRIVAL at the Menai Straits with two legions, auxiliaries and a battle fleet in the spring of A.D. 60 was graphically described by Tacitus. The Romans faced an armed mass of Celts intermingled with Druids, both men and women, shrieking curses upon them. The sight was so weird and unnerving that at first the legionnaires stood watching in terror, unable to move. This was the Druids' first important and concerted appearance upon the stage of world history. It was also to be their last.

The Romans were mustered on the beach and prepared for combat. It was not long before their military logic and discipline prevailed over druidic curses. They stormed the beaches of the mystical island. The Druids and their attendant warriors were butchered and the whole island was systematically devastated—its sacred groves put to the axe.

The victory was complete, the triumph assured, but even as Suetonius raised the cup of glory to his lips it was dashed to the ground by the arrival of a messenger who had ridden pell-mell from the south. The whole of the province had burst into flames. Boudica, queen of the Iceni, had raised the standard of revolt.

While Suetonius had been pursuing the Silures and Ordovices in the mountains and drawing the net ever tighter around the Druids on Mona, Catus, the Imperial Procurator, had been pursuing Nero's new fiscal policies with equal diligence. The emperor's edict was fresh in his mind when an unexpected opportunity to raise extra imperial revenue—and money for himself—presented itself in A.D. 60. Boudica's husband Prasutagus, king of the Iceni, had died toward the end of the previous year. He left half his huge estate to Nero and the remainder to his two daughters, in the hope that this would satisfy the emperor's greed and that his family would be left in peace. The effect was precisely the opposite. Catus saw that it gave him a pretext to sequester the whole of the dead king's estate and absorb the kingdom into the empire. Boudica resisted. She was flogged and her daughters raped, and she vowed bloody vengeance.

It was the tale of this vengeance that burst upon the victorious governor in his moment of triumph amid the ruins of the druidic groves. Boudica had raised her tribe, the neighboring Trinovantes had come to the aid of the Iceni, and they had set out for the undefended city of Colchester. The emperor's temple, the veterans' colony, everything built in seventeen years of Roman rule, had gone up in flames. The inhabitants had been butchered. The victorious mob—no one could consider it an army—was now heading for nearby London, then a new and thriving commercial center. To Suetonius it must have seemed like the Druids' revenge, the fulfillment of the disregarded curses hurled at him hours before on the beaches. Maybe he viewed it as a plot to draw him away from the implacable advance on Mona, a stratagem that had come too late. Many have suggested that the Druids organized Caratacus's resistance in the Welsh mountains, and who knows whether they had a hand in this sudden flaring of the Iceni?

Suetonius was the quintessential man of action, a seasoned commander. He made his military dispositions coolly and calmly. He then gathered his cavalry and set off for London down the course of Watling Street, leaving his two legions to follow at all speed with their baggage train in tow. Swift messengers were sent to the Second Legion's base at Gloucester, commanding the legion to meet Suetonius at High Cross, Venonis, where Watling Street crossed the Fosse Way near Leicester. The Ninth Legion, in Cambridgeshire, was ordered to move to London to contain the rebels and avert the threat to the new city.

The Roman forces were dispersed and outnumbered at the time of the revolt. Their plight was exacerbated by the fact that the Second Legion was tied down by further Silurian attacks, which may have been planned to coincide with the Icenian rebellion. For this reason, the commander of the Second Legion ignored Suetonius's order to rendezvous with him. Undaunted, Suetonius pressed on to London with only his small cavalry force. When he reached the undefended city, he was amazed to find it intact. Boudica's host had not sacked it after razing Colchester. Instead, they had turned north to meet the threat of the Ninth Legion hurrying south. Boudica had prepared a clever and devastating ambush. The news that came to Suetonius from that unknown battlefield was numbing and unbelievable: the Ninth Legion had been destroyed. Whether the victory was won through Boudica's tactics or the Britons' sheer weight of numbers we do not know. In any event, encouraged and inflamed by the success, Boudica turned now to London, which was protected only by Suetonius's small band of cavalry.

Suetonius weighed the situation calmly. He knew that his small and ill-equipped cavalry force was unlikely to prevail against the massive horde of rebellious Britons, and that the unfortified city of London was indefensible. The only hope of defeating Boudica lay in the infantry of the Fourteenth and Twentieth Legions, already on their way down Watling Street. Suetonius determined to link up with them and draw Boudica toward him for the decisive confrontation.

The strategy was an enormous gamble. Boudica could have pursued his cavalry and destroyed it rather than attacking defenseless London. But Suetonius guessed that after the battle with the Ninth Legion her seething mass of warriors would head for plunder and destruction and that she would be unable to contain them. By sacrificing London, Suetonius would buy the time he needed to regroup his forces and pick a battleground that would maximize the advantages of disciplined Roman arms. Once London had been sacked, Boudica's army was likely to crumble as the British tribesmen, sated with death and plunder, and secure in the belief that they had won, drifted back to their homes. The longer Suetonius delayed the battle, the greater were his chances of winning it. But he had to steel himself to sacrifice London, the second city of the province and a thriving trading center. It was a bitter decision. He left the city amid the clamor of the abandoned populace, taking with him only men who could serve in his cavalry force. They rode rapidly up Watling Street to keep the tryst with the advancing legions.

The gamble worked, but the cost was even greater than Suetonius feared. Boudica's army ignored his fleeing cavalry, fell upon defenseless London and put it to fire and sword. The destruction was so thorough that two thousand years later a thick layer of ash and charcoal still marks her grim passage in the archaeological record. Even then, Boudica did not seek the inevitable confrontation with

Suetonius. Instead, her army sacked Verulamium (St. Albans), twenty miles north of London. Suetonius had bought his precious time, but at appalling cost. The three main provincial cities had been destroyed and untold thousands of Britons, Romans and foreign merchants killed. The day of reckoning, however, was now approaching. The link with the two legions was effected, and the united Roman forces prepared for battle.

Suetonius knew that if he were to be defeated, Britain would be left with only one intact legion, and that tied down by the Silures. Rome's grip on Britain would be fatally weakened, and the province would become ungovernable. In A.D. 9, the loss of Varus's three legions in the battle of the Teutoburger Wald had blunted the Roman advance into Germania so thoroughly that the frontier fell back to the Rhine and never moved forward again. It was now distinctly possible that a defeat of Suetonius could place Britain forever beyond the imperial frontiers.

Much speculation surrounds the site of this final confrontation. Legend places it just north of the destroyed city of London. Tacitus says the Romans chose a narrow defile with protected flanks and a steep approach as their battleground, and it has been suggested that the village of Mancetter near High Cross, in Warwickshire, most nearly matches that topography. There is much to support this view, not least the enduring Celtic name, which means "place of the chariots."

Vastly outnumbered, with some ten thousand men against possibly eight times that number of British, Suetonius put his military judgment to the ultimate test at this most critical juncture for the fledgling province of Roman Britain. The battle swiftly turned into a rout as the British charge broke upon the Roman shields and collapsed under the hail of legionary javelins. The Romans were vengeful and implacable as the battle turned their way, and Tacitus reports a death toll of eighty thousand Britons for a few hundred Roman dead. Whether he is referring only to those killed in the battle or including those slaughtered in the sack of the three cities is unclear. Either way, with the total population of Britain estimated at around two million at that time, the effect of the slaughter would have been profound.

The late spring and early summer of A.D. 60 was a darker hour for Britain than 1066 or 1940. Three great disasters, one after another, struck down the British Celts. The Druids were shattered and the sacred groves destroyed. The defeated Queen Boudica fled from the disastrous battle and committed suicide. And the unrest caused by the rebellion, Tacitus tells us, led the farmers to abandon the planting of the spring crops.

Britain lay at the mercy of the three remaining legions, which were smarting from the destruction of the Ninth. They were headed by Suetonius, whose triumph over the Druids of Mona had been shattered by the revolt and the destruction of the cities. After the victory over Boudica, throughout the black year of A.D. 60, the legions were regrouped and reinforced for their punitive role. Suetonius then began a reign of terror over the surviving Celts. Fugitive rebels were hunted down and killed. The three cities were rebuilt and fortified, then held under iron control. Legionary fortresses and camps were built in the occupied territories, linked by arrow-straight Roman roads.

The building of the great legionary fortress of Chester dates from that time of iron retribution. It marked the line of Roman advance across the island in A.D. 60. From then on, Rome's hold was consolidated and pushed ever further northward and westward, starting in A.D. 71 under Agricola's governorship. The only real chance of defeating the Romans had gone. They reigned supreme over a devastated country that faced famine because of the neglected fields.

This, then, was the darkest hour in Britain's blackest year. The Celts had suffered the triple loss of the druidic sanctuary, the harvest and the warriors. They had fought three legions, annihilating one, being annihilated by the other two. And the Romans had lost three cities. There was no end in sight to the dark, cruel night of Roman rule. The gods had deserted the Celts. In this blackest of hours it was time for their holiest sacrifice to be made, for the vengeful gods to be placated. For this, we believe, Lovernios died and entered the pool, to sleep within the sacred waters until the Roman night had passed.

NO MAN'S LAND

WE HAVE ALREADY identified the sacrifice of Lovernios as a Beltain event. The highly unusual form of the sacrifice, which brings together the *devoted one* and the *divine victim* in one person, suggests that this was an extraordinary Beltain feast, one that marked a time when hope for the future, and the good will of the gods, were almost dead. Up to that year, there had been no certainty that the Romans would prevail: the Cambrian tribes were undefeated and the great sanctuary on Mona was secure and unviolated. At the end of Suetonius's campaign, the sanctuary was destroyed and the shattered province was in the grip of terror and famine.

After Beltain of A.D. 60 there was no further prospect of rebellion, no hope that the merciless Romans, now reinforced by two thousand legionnaires and other auxiliary troops from the empire, would ever be overthrown by British force of arms. And it was unlikely that a sacred druidic ceremony could be carried out with impunity in the heavily policed Roman domains.

It was against this bleak background that the significance of Lindow Moss as the sacrificial site at last became apparent. It was chosen because it was the only suitable hidden place left in the maelstrom of Roman activity that swept through the area, for it was in an unfrequented no man's land. Lindow Moss lies in a narrow triangle of land between the Roman military frontier established by Suetonius's move toward Anglesey from the south and the borders of the client kingdom of the Brigantes to the north. It has been suggested that in the immediate aftermath of the rebellion, this triangle was a forward military zone, cleared of population and subject to military laws and patrol, but outside the established frontier based upon the fort of Chester. Any large druidic gathering at the sacred feast time of Beltain was impossible south of this frontier, for it would have attracted Roman attention. And any move into Brigantia might bring betrayal, as it had to Caratacus. The natural hiding place in the marshes of Lindow Moss was the only place left. The black year reached its nadir at the Black Lake, and it was here that the supreme sacrifice was made.

Careful inspection of the evidence shows how events moved remorselessly toward that bitter climax at Beltain. The death of the Icenian King Prasutagus, which precipitated the Boudican revolt, occurred in the winter of A.D. 59–60. It may be assumed that Catus moved in on his estates shortly afterward. For news of the revolt to have reached Suetonius at the moment of his triumph on Anglesey, the roads must have been fit for traveling and that implies early

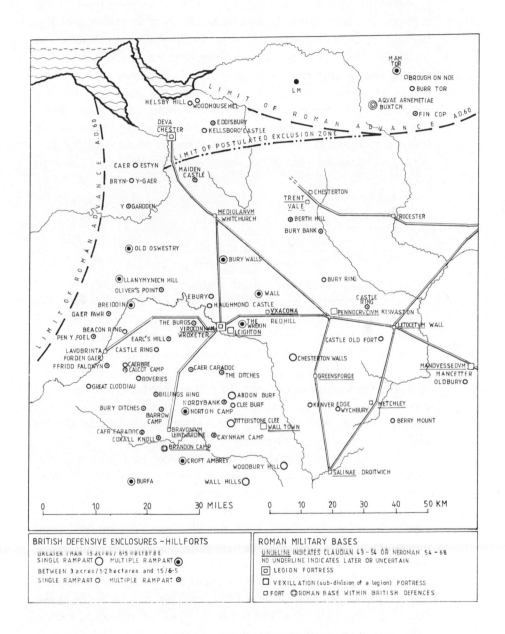

Iron Age and Roman places in and around Cornovia, with Roman roads. The
Limit of the Roman Advance by A.D. 60 and the Restricted Zone between the
Chester area and the northern limit of the Advance are shown.

spring (Watling Street north of High Cross was then outside the military frontier). Since Beltain is at the end of spring and the beginning of summer, this places the sacrifice after the destruction on Mona, after the news of the abandonment of the fields. The gloomy Beltain feast must have taken place when most of the Roman troops were still in the south or Midlands after the great battle at Mancetter. So a secret gathering and ceremony would have been possible in a secluded place such as Lindow where there was no immediate threat of Roman reprisals. Lindow Moss, with its dark pools and lakes, was chosen because there were few other places to go.

THE TERROR

IN A.D. 61, THE SITUATION in the country, after a winter of terror and famine, would have been still worse. However, the likelihood of holding such a druidic ceremony even in Lindow Moss would have been more remote, given the increasing Roman presence in Chester, *unless it took place with the Romans' knowledge.*

This is a possibility that is worth exploring. The Romans hated druidism, and we have seen how they desecrated and destroyed the sacred groves on Mona. It seems more than likely that their hatred, after the revolt, might have led to persecution of surviving Druids and the mocking of their most sacred ceremonies.

We call to mind the Roman treatment of Christ and the severity and often mocking cruelty of Roman punishment in general. The Roman role in the crucifixion of Christ is not easy to interpret; but crucifixion as a form of execution derived from a Carthaginian sacrificial rite that the Romans adopted and used mockingly against their defeated enemies. Later they applied it widely to low-class and non-Roman felons. Christ himself was mocked as a Jewish king by the crown of thorns and the inscription INRI. The Roman treatment of Christ can be seen as the degradation of a fallen king. And the mockery of Christ occurred a mere generation before the death of Lovernios.

Could they have treated Lovernios in similar fashion? The Roman soldiers were expert killers and executioners, adept at copying their enemies' methods to strike terror into the vanquished.

Could they have forced this bizarre death upon a surviving Druid as an ultimate sacrilege, a parody of the order's deepest beliefs about human sacrifice?

There were two objections to this argument. One was that everything pointed to a Beltain feast and sacrifice, where Lovernios took the blackened piece. We considered it unlikely that the Romans would have gone to these lengths in their mockery of the Druids. The other was that a Roman mockery of the Beltain ceremony would not need to be conducted in the secrecy of the marshes in the no man's land of the military zone. If mockery and sacrilege were the reason for his death, the record of Roman punishment suggested that this would have been a very public, rather than a private, death. The coincidence of so many Celtic factors hinted that it was a cry of despair at the ruin of Britain under the Roman hand.

So how did Lovernios die, and how was he chosen? How was the sacrifice conducted? The hypothesis that we now put forward, though of necessity conjectural, accounts for all the key elements in the death of Lindow Man that have so far been deduced.

THE DEVOTED ONE

IF THE CEREMONY was secret, we must suppose it took place at night. The Celts reckoned in nights, not days, and we suggest that the Beltain Eve was marked by the moonrise over the no man's land of the marshes.

Would the ceremony have taken place beside the Black Lake or the somber pool? We think that unlikely. There is nothing to indicate that Lindow was a special or sacred place until this status was forced upon it by the events of the black year. Even given the secrecy of the sacrifice, it is unlikely that the participants would have conducted it at an unhallowed place. Our feeling, after visiting the Lindow area, is that the most likely location of the sacred site is Alderley Edge, perhaps close to the well, or on its highest point. Hilltop bonfires were the most conspicuous feature of traditional Beltain, but in this inauspicious year they would have attracted the attention of the Romans. A glade on the heavily wooded hilltop seems the most likely site for the ceremony. Nearby Mobberley, the name of which also indicates a forest clearing, is a possible contender; so is Wilmslow, whose name signifies an ancient burial mound. Bronze Age remains have been found close by Wilmslow church, and the archaeology of Alderley Edge goes back to the late Stone Ages.

Wherever it took place, the criteria remain the same: a sacred site, a grove or well (or both), almost certainly within a mile of the final resting place, perhaps linked to it by a wooden causeway where a woodland track petered out into the marshes. The pollen evidence points to a sodden landscape, where a causeway might have sunk below the surface, a place where heavily laden Roman troops would not have ventured willingly. The grove must have been close to heathland, source of the heather leaves in the sacred pancake; its trees would have masked the smoke from the fire that cooked the pancake.

There would have been no great bonfires on that desperate and gloomy Beltain, when crops were not planted and livestock was sequestered by the Romans. But a small fire to cook the sacred pancake from the grain of the previous harvest was all that was necessary. Were the pieces placed in the leathern bag and shared between the celebrants, the black mark indicating the sacrifice? Or did Lovernios offer himself? Had he already been chosen?

Here we confront the central mystery of the sacrifice on Lindow Moss. If the ceremony followed the black spring, if the Druids were slaughtered in their stronghold on Mona, who were the celebrants? Even if Lovernios had not been a Druid himself, his executioners were skilled in the techniques of sacrifice and were undoubtedly members of the druidic order. But our deductions show that Lovernios *was* a Druid, and his body provides no evidence that he went through desperate battles on Mona before being consigned to his watery grave. We recall again the uncannily unblemished appearance of his body, almost as if he had waited for the moment of sacrifice all his life. Placing this in the context of the black spring, with its turmoil and destruction, we can approach the question of the identity of Lovernios.

If he had come from Gaul before moving into Wales ahead of the Roman advance, his journey would probably have taken him to Anglesey, and it is hard to believe that he would have escaped the holocaust unscathed when Suetonius attacked. It seems more likely that Lovernios came from Ireland in Britain's darkest hour. We

ABOVE *The Celtic god Cernunnos, antlered and squatting, from one of the inner plates of the silver cauldron found in Gundestrup, Jutland, Denmark*

BELOW *Cernunnos, brandishing a stag in either hand, from one of the outer plates of the Gundestrup cauldron*

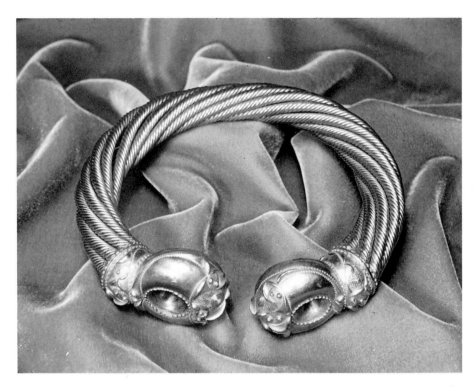

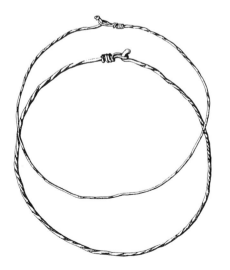

ABOVE *Gold torc, found in Snettisham, Norfolk*

LEFT *Bronze torcs, found in Celtic sanctuary at Libenice, Czechoslovakia*

TOP RIGHT *Wooden tricethalos in Llandinam Church, Monmouthshire (Gwent)*

RIGHT *Three-headed torso, with central head bearing a torc and holes for antlers, found at Condat, Dordogne, France*

0 1 2 3cm

Stone head of a one-eyed god, possibly the Irish deity Balor

Bronze Celtic shield recovered from River Thames at Battersea, London

Celtic stone head found in Chester, Cheshire

One of several Celtic stone heads found in Glossop, Derbyshire

LEFT *Celtic stone head found in Wilmington, East Sussex*

BELOW *Sandstone statue of Celtic god wearing a torc and emblazoned with a boar, Euffigneix, Haute-Marne, France*

TOP LEFT *Bronze model cult-wagon bearing a goddess, spearmen, axemen with female companions, and a stag between a pair of human figures, seventh century BC, found in Austria*

ABOVE *Dressed Well, Saddleworth, Lancashire*

LEFT *The Antler Dance, Abbots Bromley, Staffordshire*

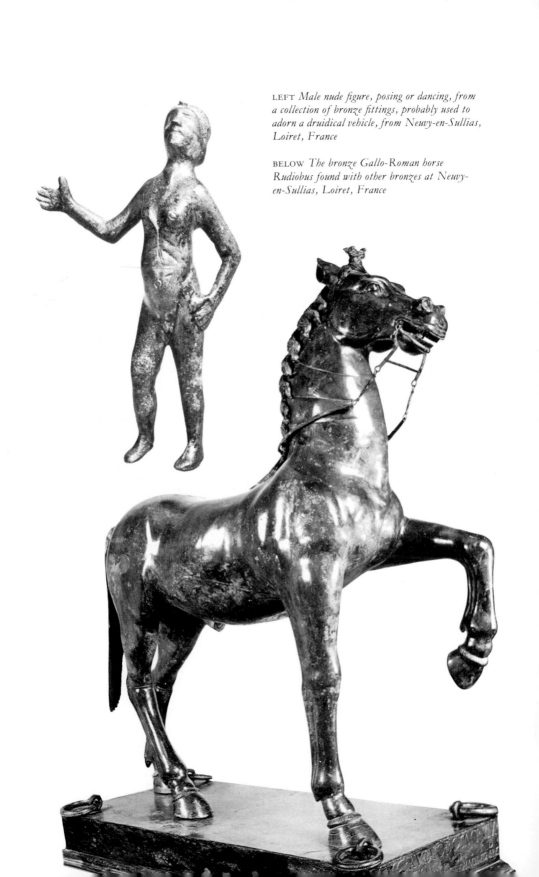

LEFT *Male nude figure, posing or dancing, from a collection of bronze fittings, probably used to adorn a druidical vehicle, from Neuvy-en-Sullias, Loiret, France*

BELOW *The bronze Gallo-Roman horse Rudiobus found with other bronzes at Neuvy-en-Sullias, Loiret, France*

describe the role of Ireland—as the *insula sacra*, the sacred island—
in the fate and survival of druidism in Appendix 1. While Lovernios's Irish origin cannot be established with certainty, his unblemished appearance and kingly rank suggest that he would not
have been involved in the slaughter in Mona, and may indeed have
arrived after it had finished.

If he had traveled from Ireland, sailing up the Mersey, the
boundary river, into the Bollin, he might well have reached Lindow
unscathed. Perhaps he was originally intended as a counterweight to
the Roman assault on Mona, but arrived too late on the Welsh coast
to influence events. His entourage, accompanied possibly by fugitive Druids from the Welsh mountains, then converged upon the no
man's land of Lindow Moss to make the awful sacrifice. If this
scenario is anywhere near correct, it goes a long way toward
answering one of our most persistent questions. Was he chosen by
the lottery of the pancake, or had his death already been ordained?

Lovernios, having witnessed the destruction of the British
Druids, could not simply return to a now vulnerable Ireland. His
high rank fitted him for this supreme sacrifice. Perhaps the day and
manner of his death, and the reason for it, had been prophesied.
Our earlier suspicions were confirmed: that Lovernios knew he was
going to die and composed himself for the solemn and somber
occasion. When the pancake was baked, he took the blackened slice.

If this explanation was correct, it answered a question raised by
the scientific analysis. The scorch mark was very small, much
smaller than might be expected, perhaps just enough to see by the
flickering light of the fire or the moon hanging over the treetops.
Was it enough to pick out the *devoted one* and the *divine victim* in
one?

RIDING THE LORD

OUR UNRAVELING of the story of Lovernios, his life and his death,
now came full circle. We started by analyzing his death. From that
we deduced his life and the reason for his death. Now we could look
again at the evidence of his sacrifice and see the ceremony with fresh
eyes.

We have already stated that we do not think Lovernios died at

Lindow but rather at a sacred grove in the military zone, either at Mobberley or on Alderley Edge. The evidence for his kneeling to receive the axe blows to the crown of his head is compelling, and demonstrates his calm acquiescence in the ritual death. That the final blow to the head was delivered to his supine body also seems self-evident. Taranis's share of the sacrifice was over swiftly.

The garroting and slitting of the jugular now required a new appraisal. We knew that the garroting killed Lovernios almost instantly and that the jugular was slit on the point of death. It seemed likely that the executioner—who may have been one of the lower orders of Druids, the Vates—brought the garrote into play when the unconscious Lovernios had been propped up in a sitting or kneeling position. The action of the garrote requires considerable exertion to produce the killing twist with the stick and cord. It was likely that the executioner obtained that exertion by jamming his knee with great force into Lovernios's back and pulling against the spine while the body was held. This fierce action could account for the broken ribs; it also raises an interesting problem concerning Lovernios's posture in death.

Inspection of the body, as recovered from the peat, shows the torso in a semi-crouching attitude, with the remains of the arms in a leaning position. At first we, along with other commentators, thought this posture indicated that the execution was performed at the side of the pool, after which the body was allowed to fall into the water. Our theory of a nearby sacred site as the venue for the ceremony made that seem unlikely. There was also the practical consideration that this carefully coordinated and violent sequence of actions would have been difficult if the participants were standing in a peat bog.

We surmised that after the third axe blow to the base of the skull, the unconscious Lovernios was hauled upright, with one priest holding each arm. He would then have been placed on a stool or similar backless seat while the Vates arranged the garrote around his neck. Since the bleedings from the jugular took place during the garroting but started after it had begun, Lovernios would also have been arranged for that gruesome process before the garroting.

The sacred bloodletting, we felt, made sense in the Celtic context only if the blood was drained into a *caldron*, the quintessential Celtic vessel of lore and magic. Lovernios, then, was sitting upright, his head hanging over a caldron and his limp arms resting on his knees, while the Vates tightened the garrote. At the correct moment, the Vates's assistant stabbed into the throat and released the jet of blood into the caldron. Thus was Esus, lord and master, placated.

Lovernios would have been held in this position until the blood drained completely and his head flopped down into the hollow of his right shoulder. The onset of rigor mortis would have started to freeze his limbs into their leaning position before the caldron of sacred blood was removed and the final grim journey could commence.

Here we are reminded of local folklore again, "riding the lord" and "riding the black lad." Perhaps the dead Lovernios was lifted on to a white horse—or placed in a chariot drawn by white horses? Either way, his sitting posture would have been a fitting one for the journey.

This powerful image of the sacrificed Lovernios being drawn in a chariot, down a trackway through the thick woods of the sacred hill toward the moss, has strong undertones of another Celtic ritual. In times of disaster, the Celts—and the Germans—would parade the image of their great goddess Anu (called Nerthus by the Germans) around the fields in a special chariot, the Anoniredi. She would be accompanied by her consort, and the people would flock to her, clamoring for her blessing. During his journey in the chariot from the sacred grove to the pool where Teutates awaited to claim him, Lovernios might well have been accompanied by the image of Anu. In this moment of solemn sacrifice, the *divine victim* would become the consort of the great earth mother.

Perhaps the celebrants and the frightened and horror-struck onlookers followed the slow progress of the chariot to the pool, beseeching the goddess for her mercy and the gods for their forgiveness. Each of the gods had his sacrifice in Lovernios's death. Sitting beside the goddess, in her chariot, on his final journey, Lovernios was the divine victim coming down from his own oak-grove calvary.

Or perhaps the crowd execrated him as the Beltain scapegoat, leaving a residual memory that lingered on in the "riding the lord" ceremonies. But in that moonlight, on the spectral marshes, they would have been awed by the solemnity of the occasion and fear of the future. Their curses would have been muted. Close by the chosen pool, the *devoted one* would have been lifted from the chariot and placed reverently in the care of the god of the people, Teutates. They would have watched as the body sank below the surface of the dark waters and disappeared. The king had gone into the ground; in time the earth would close above him, the guardian of the faith.

The reign of terror passed, the Romans built their towns and their roads. Centuries later, their power waned; then the English came. But still this area of England remained stubbornly Celtic. A hedge of silence, differing customs, alien thoughts, kept the memory of Lovernios alive.

When we reached this somber point in our quest we paused, wondering whether there was still a piece of the jigsaw puzzle missing. One doubt nagged insistently: why did the Romans persecute the Druids so implacably, although the priesthood was clearly no match for their political power and diplomatic skill? Was there some real druidic power that the Romans were determined to break, some druidic treasure they were determined to seize? What could the Druids have possessed that the Romans wanted so desperately?

If the black year gave the Romans what they wanted, if they wrested something of great value from the Druids in that year as well as visiting devastation upon them, there might be yet another layer of symbolism and meaning in Lovernios's death. It was the Alderley legend that provided the elusive clue to the final stage of our quest.

CHAPTER SIX

THE GOLDEN
TWIST

THE DEATH OF LOVERNIOS in A.D. 60 was, we believe, triggered by
the three great disasters of that year. His sacrifice at Beltain was the
high point of British druidism, the culmination of the Romans'
ruthless campaign against the order and the beginning of the long
and bitter night under the Roman heel. However, Suetonius's reign
of terror which followed that crushing of Boudica's revolt was short-
lived. It was soon replaced by a milder regime that gradually
restored British prosperity and left the Celtic religions to flourish
unmolested, although without the public stewardship of the Druids.
We still had a suspicion that the three great disasters were not so
catastrophic that the Druids could not have recovered at least some
semblance of their religious role. Were they just the outward sign of
a far greater catastrophe that dwarfed the immediate horror?

As we followed the faint clues, we began to see the story of
Boudica's rebellion from a new and unexpected angle. Lovernios's
death seemed no longer just to mark its bitter end, but to be
connected also with its cause. It has long been surmised that the
Druids had a hand in organizing Boudica's revolt. Our own suspicions now began to crystallize around two key aspects of the
rebellion that finally pointed the way to the fundamental mystery
behind the black year, and to the ultimate cause of Lovernios's
death.

Our questions centered around Boudica in particular and the
Iceni in general. They were directed at details of the sparse Roman
narrative that are always repeated but rarely questioned. Why, we

wondered, was her husband so rich? His enormous wealth had triggered Catus's cupidity and the slighting of Boudica that caused the revolt. Why had Catus acted with such savagery and greed against the Iceni?

The questions multiplied. Why had Boudica's army been routed so easily in the final battle? Was it simply a result of Suetonius's careful choice of battlefield and tactics, or was his choice of killing ground guided by other, subtler principles, ones that would cause Boudica's army to lose cohesion and fall easy prey to the legionnaires' javelins and short swords? Or had he stumbled upon the key to the rebels' undoing by chance? We became convinced that the key issue was why Suetonius chose Mancetter for his battlefield.

THE PLACE OF CHARIOTS

INFORMATION ABOUT Boudica's last battle, as we have seen, is extremely sparse. What exists is biased toward the Roman viewpoint, and against that of the vanquished Britons. The location of the final battlefield at Mancetter, near Nuneaton, was not proven, although we found the arguments for it extremely convincing. But was Suetonius's choice of battleground based purely upon military logic? Could Mancetter have been a sacred place of the Celts, and did Suetonius choose it to goad them into desperation and blind fury? If it was sacred, we might discern a druidic connection, something that would perhaps link it directly to Lovernios.

Tacitus is our sole authority on the rebellion, and his interest is purely military. There are, however, a few telling asides. He says, for instance, that Boudica released a sacred hare between the armies before the battle commenced, the mark of a priestess seeking augury. He also describes how Boudica's followers horribly mutilated the dead—especially Roman women—during the destruction of London. These Roman matrons were not casually butchered, they were sacrificed to the bloodthirsty Celtic goddess Andraste, and Boudica is described as her priestess.

Was Boudica both queen and priestess? Both female and male Druids, as we saw, lined the shore on Mona and hurled curses at the Romans. Celtic ruling queens included Cartimandua of the Brigantes, who handed Caratacus over in chains. She was a powerful client of the Romans; and Boudica herself readily assumed the mantle of leadership from her husband. Perhaps a queen so powerful *had* to be a Druidess as well. That could account for the strength and ferocity of Boudica's revolt, with its careful strategy and marshaling of forces which even the Romans grudgingly admired. It may be that the druidic force behind the rebellion came from Boudica herself.

This supposition helps to explain how she was able to exert such iron control over her huge army. We recall how, after the sack of Colchester, she turned aside from the easy prey of defenseless London to face, and destroy, the Ninth Legion. Then, tracking Suetonius's flight northward up Watling Street, Boudica and her army razed St. Albans before confidently coming to grips with the Romans. The confidence is shown in the large number of families and camp followers that trailed after the army. From the beginning to the end Boudica's campaign was marked by the skill of a cool and competent strategist, a worthy opponent for Suetonius. Yet when the final showdown came, the Celts proved to be a disorganized rabble, which the Romans easily overcame.

The conventional explanation of this collapse, and of the slaughter that followed, is that Boudica's control over her motley groups of warbands was slipping. Yet this was the very point when one more victory would have practically wiped out the Roman presence in Britain. Was it really the sack of the two cities that caused the army to degenerate into squabbling warbands, as Suetonius hoped and intended, or had he another ace to play in his choice of the final killing ground? We went to Mancetter in the search for clues.

From the south, its thickly wooded ridge is prominent on the horizon once High Cross is passed. Although there is little to show the earlier significance of High Cross nowadays, at that time it was the junction of Watling Street and the Fosse Way, the military pivot of early Roman Britain. The Fosse Way, stretching from Cirencester to Lincoln and beyond, was the original Roman frontier almost until Suetonius's time, and it is marked to this day by long, arrow-straight stretches of the A46 highway. Watling Street, which runs almost due west across the Midland Plain here until it reaches Wroxeter, linked to Chester and Holyhead; it survives as the A5 highway.

In Suetonius's time, the Fosse Way was already an important linking road between the frontier posts that would grow into cities such as Cirencester and Lincoln. Its diagonal lines from the Severn to the Wash defined the boundary between the occupied southeast and the unconquered Midlands and northwest. Both roads were military links for the rapid movement of legions along the frontiers. The westward extension of Watling Street is closely connected to Suetonius's push into North Wales, when he set out to crush the druidic stronghold on Anglesey.

At Mancetter, Watling Street runs close to the River Anker, under a thickly wooded hill. The London-Manchester railway line crosses the old main road, which climbs up the flank of the hill through Atherstone as a long, straight main street. This is the most likely site of the battle, with the Romans flanked by wooded hillside to the right and river to the left. Mancetter church, at the foot of the hill, is the reputed site of a Roman fort of Claudian date (A.D. 43–54).

Was there an important Celtic shrine on the Mancetter heights that the Romans destroyed as they took up their defensive positions? A thickly wooded hill might well have had a sacred grove or spring, but no evidence has been found so far for any such site at Mancetter. Was the river itself sacred? The name Anker is a Celtic name meaning "winding river." In the present case, however, our search had to be for something out of the ordinary; the presence of a sacred grove, spring or river was not enough in itself. The search did not take long. A few miles north of the battlefield was one of the greatest sacred sites of Celtic Britain.

VERNEMETON

MANCETTER IS ONE of the names on the map of modern Britain that echo the Celtic heritage buried beneath the Roman, Saxon, Viking, Norman and English overlay. The name of the Roman fort on the site was Mandvessedum, and subsequent conquerors have merely softened the unfamiliar syllables. Unlike river names, most urban Celtic place names have not survived at all into our times; we know of them only through chance survivals of Roman documentation.

Such a chance identifies the great Celtic sanctuary of Vernemeton, twenty-five miles northeast of Mancetter, which was occupied for a now unknown period before becoming Romanized after the conquest. There are now no surface remains of the "great grove" beside the Fosse Way, and so you will not find Vernemeton on the Ordnance Survey landranger series (number 129) map. It has been excavated cursorily over the years, but remains little known even to archaeologists. To reach it from Mancetter you must follow the straight line of the Fosse Way due northeast. Much of the Roman road's course survives as the A46 highway, which leads through Leicester, the old Romano-British city of Ratae. Fourteen miles beyond Leicester, the Fosse Way changes course slightly as it goes over the brow of a little hill. There the ancient county boundaries of Leicestershire and Nottinghamshire meet, and a minor road leads off to the village of Willoughby-on-the-Wolds. This junction on the crest is the site of Vernemeton, which lay on the western slope of the hill.

Since the eighteenth century, stretches of tesselated pavements, foundations and coins have been found from time to time on the slope, in what is known as the Black Field. Much of the blackness had been ascribed to huge ancient fires. These few scattered finds are all that has come to light of the sacred site of Vernemeton. Its closeness to the Fosse Way suggested that the Romans may have driven the road contemptuously through the sacred site, as they did further south between the sacred springs and shrines in Bath.

Did Suetonius desecrate and burn this sacred site to draw the queen-priestess northward to the killing ground, the "place of chariots"? The proximity of the two sites, battlefield and grove, and their linking by the Fosse Way, hint at a shared significance. The Fosse Way, after all, was not simply a Roman invention: it marked the great geographical divide of Britain between southeastern lowlands and northwestern uplands that has dominated Britain's development for centuries. The brutal line of the road reinforced the sense of a frontier; this sense persists even today if you stand by the A46 highway and look westward across the Midland Plain toward the distant mountains.

Vernemeton is not the only Celtic site that lies on the Fosse Way in the area where the battle was fought. Between it and Mancetter the road passes through Dane Hills. This is now a concreted suburb of Leicester, but was long associated with worship of the Celtic goddess Anu. In folklore she became the grisly Black Annis, the iron-clawed, child-eating hag who lived in the hill.

Following the line of the Fosse Way southwest of Mancetter, we come upon an enigmatic place called the Lunt, in Baginton, on the outskirts of Coventry. This is now famous for a remarkable reconstruction of a Roman fort that stood on the site, with massive wooden gateways, towers and walls. But the Lunt is not noteworthy for that alone. Among the foundations of the eastern perimeter of the fortress, the remains of a circular enclosure, 107 feet in diameter, were unearthed. It has been reconstructed in heavy timber as a vast corral, or *gyrus*. This is said to have been used for the breaking-in of horses, but it brought to mind a gladiatorial arena more than anything else.

The *gyrus* remained a puzzle. It is dated to A.D. 64–68 and one theory holds that it was built to contain the horses captured after the battle at Mancetter. The *gyrus* predates the fort and was probably never part of it. In fact, it was likely to have been a ceremonial Celtic site, like Vernemeton, that came beneath the Roman heel in the wake of the rebellion. This date, recently ascertained, provided a very convincing piece of evidence for our historical context.

If the *gyrus* was Celtic, an association with the horse would seem probable, for the Celts worshiped and revered the horse. That did not accord with the reconstruction of the circular structure as a simple corral, however. It was much more likely that the Lunt was a ceremonial center, perhaps a place where sacred races were run, or dances or rites performed with horses.

Gradually it emerged that the Fosse Way was strung with sacred and special sites on either side of the final battlefield. There was a growing sense that Mancetter, the place of chariots, was a focal point in the sacred Celtic landscape of Britain, that it stood at the center of a web whose strands we were just beginning to perceive. Suetonius blundered into the center of this web and brought Boudica and her army—charging, enraged and disorganized— toward the waiting swords and javelins of the legions.

The sacredness of these sites was one feature of the web; another was that they were linked by key Roman roads that crossed near Mancetter. Perhaps, we reasoned, the significance of Mancetter would become clearer if we looked at the sites that lay along Watling Street near the junction with Fosse Way at High Cross. Watling Street led westward from High Cross and Mancetter, then swung west and north across the land of the Cornovii. It passed through Chester, close by Lindow Moss, and ended on Anglesey, the holy island of the Druids. Beyond that was Ireland, the *insula sacra* of the Celts. If Lovernios had come from Ireland to his sacrifice, as we believed, he would have trodden part of this route on his way to Lindow Moss. And if we had divined his purpose correctly, it was already a hallowed and sacred way.

Lindow, Mancetter, the Lunt, Vernemeton, Mona, the Dane Hills—what else linked this Celtic web to the final battle and the coming of Roman rule? By examining the paths of the Roman roads, we had found a thread connecting all these places to the catastrophe of the black year. The thread was golden, twisted from many strands. It was made from the gold of Ireland, the *insula sacra*. And it identified a Celtic route studded with temples.

THE GOLDEN THREAD

WEST OF MANCETTER and Vernemeton, Watling Street passes through the Trent–Severn passage. This gap is some twenty-five miles wide, defined on the southern edge by the River Severn and to the north by the line of the River Trent, which curves past the flanks of the Derbyshire hills. Between Mancetter and Chester, the future site of the great Roman fortress of Deva, lie two Roman fortifications dating from the earliest stage of Suetonius's advance northward. Each of these marks an important British site on an ancient route from the Midlands through the Trent–Severn passage to the sanctuary of Anglesey and thence to Ireland.

Unlike the Fosse Way, which marked a geographical divide, Watling Street strung together a line of such British settlements. Among the more interesting are the two immediately to the north of Mancetter—and thus south of Lindow—at Penkridge and Wall. Like Mancetter, these fortifications date from the Neronian phase of the conquest (after A.D. 54).

Both Penkridge and Wall were important Celtic religious sites—they were sacred groves set in dense woodland. Wall, the Roman Letocetum—the "gray wood"—was the site of a great pagan temple to Minerva, the Romanized form of the Celtic goddess Brigit, whose name is still written large upon the British landscape. Several Celtic horned stone heads and carved slabs were found at Wall. Their distinctive motifs link them to the Celtic tribes in what is

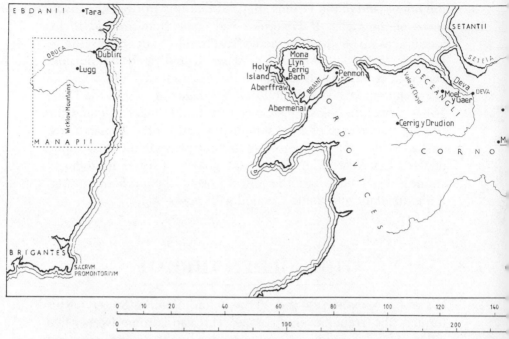

The Gold Route, showing Ireland to the west and Denmark to the east.

now Derbyshire (where the county symbol is still the ram). Abbots Bromley, where the famous antler-bearing dancers perform to this day, is only eleven miles north of Wall.

Penkridge, twelve miles west of Wall, is nowadays a small village. The name implies a ridge of slight hill and its Roman form, Pennocrucium, is a rendering of the Celtic "head of the mound" or "chief mound." There is no hill close by and we saw the name as indicating an assembly-place centered upon a grave mound. The ancient significance hidden in Penkridge's present name was the first tentative link we found between the battleground of Mancetter and the sacrifice of Lovernios at Lindow Moss.

The name Pennocrucium is the British equivalent of the Gaelic Cenn Croich, the god of the harvest in Ireland, otherwise known as Crom Dubh, the "dark bent one." This sinister, destroying god was said to oppose the young, shining god of the harvest, Lugh. The name Pennocrucium may associate Penkridge, and possibly the nearby gray wood of Letocetum with the worship of this fearsome deity but we saw its importance in another way. The slight but

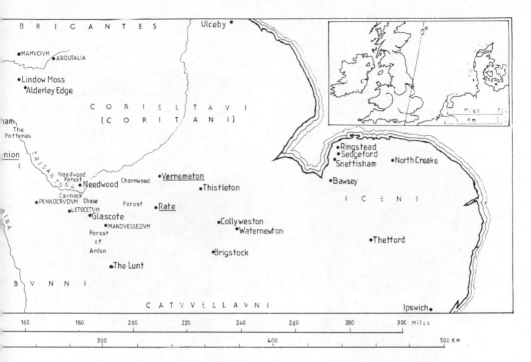

tangible link with Ireland, the concept of a destroying god and
Penkridge's proximity to areas of Derbyshire and Cheshire where
we had noted an enduring Celtic presence, all indicated that the line
of Watling Street marked a corridor of druidic influence.

Watling Street, as we have seen, cuts through the Trent–
Severn passage to Wroxeter before heading north to Chester and
then around the coast of North Wales to Anglesey. In linking sites
such as Mancetter, Penkridge and Wall, and driving between
Vernemeton and the *gyrus* of the Lunt, Watling Street reveals itself
as the Roman overlay of an ancient Celtic route marked by holy
places. This runs through the Trent–Severn passage to the Vale of
Clwyd and thence across the Menai Straits to Anglesey.

If it was not just a sacred way linking holy sites, it was controlled
or used by the Druids for some other purpose. The idea of a sacred
Celtic highway is not new: there are several known parallels with
royal roads and sacred ways.

If the road was restricted to druidic use, or controlled by the
Druids for their own purposes, where did it lead from Anglesey? To

answer this question we had to look more closely at Anglesey. Our attention, so far, had been concentrated upon the Menai Straits where the Druids met the Roman onslaught with their blood-curdling curses. The Roman road crosses these straits, passes across the island to Valley, then spans a narrow tidal strait to reach the very tip of Anglesey, a small second island now called Holy Island. Holyhead, the terminus of Watling Street, is marked by a third-century Roman fort, now called Caer Gybi (Holyhead). Beyond it is Ireland, which the Romans never reached with military force.

If a traveler took ship at Holyhead, his landfall would be Dublin. Here we noted a curious correspondence. The Celtic roots of the name "Dublin" are the same as those of Lindow—they both mean "black lake." What else might connect the two places, bearing in mind our suspicion that Lindow Man came from Ireland?

Just beyond Dublin lie the Wicklow hills. Here was the prime source of the pale Irish gold of the ancient tales. It was not just a legendary metal, however, for the working of Irish gold was the crowning glory of Celtic craftsmanship and art, one of the great wonders of the ancient world. Ireland was a font of druidism and gold, which were both exported to the mainland of Europe through

These two altars from Alpraham, near Chester, are made of sandstone, probably from the Keuper beds of central Cheshire. Because of its crumbly texture, this stone does not weather well, and evidence of this can be seen in the poor condition of much of the detail of the heads and the creatures that occur in relief on the fronts and backs of the stones. Each altar is roughly ten inches wide and sixteen inches tall, with a well-defined *focus* on the top.

The striations on the forehead, cheeks, and chin of the faces may represent tattooing or face-painting. The details of the four eyes have suffered from erosion, but a shallow, circular depression is clearly marked at the inner end of each eye socket. On both faces the lips are drawn back to reveal teeth.

The creature on the back of the top altar, placed sideways on the stone but with the face looking vertically, is probably a bull: the remains of horns and a tuft of curled hair on the top of the head can be distinguished. The creature on the other altar, unfortunately badly damaged, crouches on its belly with all four legs pointing forward, heading up the stone. The remains of eyes are visible, and what is probably the left-hand extremity of the mouth, but the snout has been broken off, as have much of the left foreleg and the rear hind legs. Shallow striations across the back can be seen where the surface has not worn away.

While these creatures are unparalleled, as far as has been discovered, in works of this kind, their likeness to the principal features on the base of the Gundestrup caldron is striking. The prone bull on the caldron faces a creature in the position adopted by the Alpraham beast, the only marked difference being the lack of a tail in the latter.

Britain. Watling Street, marching through the Trent–Severn gap, hugging the coastal strip of North Wales, rolling on to the very tip of Anglesey, now stood revealed in a stark and unusual light. It did not just mark Celtic ritual sites and sanctuaries, important as these undoubtedly were, and it was not only a relic of Suetonius's campaign and its aftermath.

The line of Watling Street marked above all a *trade route*, a Celtic trade route based upon the flow of gold from Ireland to Britain, continental Europe and beyond. The trade was organized and controlled by the Druids, whose sanctuaries lined its route. If this identification of the gold route was anything like correct, the Roman assault on Anglesey appeared in a new light. Beyond the Roman claim that Anglesey was the key supply base for the Ordovician and Silurian resistance, which had to be eliminated at any cost, we now saw another factor that the Romans never mentioned. Anglesey was the pivot of druidic wealth, and this was expressed in gold. In striking at Anglesey, they accomplished much more than the destruction of the druidic sanctuary; they broke the economic power of the Druids. But did the Romans know what they had accomplished?

The fabled wealth of Britain had persuaded the Romans to invade in the first place. They had committed four legions, withdrawn from sensitive frontiers, to a campaign beyond the confines of the known world of their time, and they expected a handsome return on their investment. The wealth of the southern kingdoms and their exporting of cattle, grain, hunting dogs and slaves were famed in the Roman world, as was the workmanship of the Celtic craftsmen. The latter could be sustained only by the patronage of a wealthy aristocracy, the extent of whose wealth—always displayed most flamboyantly in gold—was very great.

The most costly objects were made not for everyday use but for display and ritual—which may have been the same thing. Many of the finest seem to have been intended specifically for throwing into lakes, rivers and streams as offerings for the gods and goddesses. Indeed, the second flowering of Celtic culture is named La Tène after the find of a huge deposit of wonderful and costly objects in the shallows of a Swiss lake.

The mainspring of Celtic wealth, documented by classical authors and Irish texts, and confirmed by the findings of archaeologists, was the exploitation of gold. The Druids would have closely

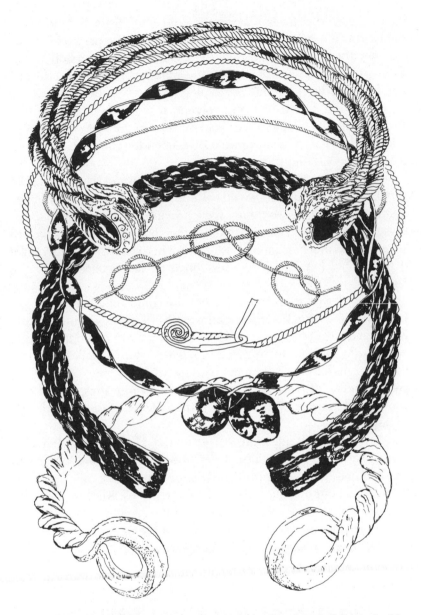

The sliding noose described as a garrote, which was found around the neck of the body in Lindow Moss, was arranged as in the formalized, loosened display in this figure. The other objects are gold torques. The top one is a multistrand example from Needwood, Staffordshire; the second a narrow torque, like a cord, from Tara, county Meath; the third a ribbon torque with acorn terminals from Clonmacnoise, County Offaly. Below the garrote is a multistrand torque from Glascote, Staffordshire, and at the bottom a torque from Ipswich, Suffolk.

controlled its distribution along the gold route from Ireland. Suddenly, this emerging scenario showed us *why* the principal fate of the metal was votive: its use by the Celts was *always* a holy thing. Perhaps even the wonders of Celtic metalworking were also dictated by druidic rules and were solely religious in their inception, execution and use. If we were correct, it was easy to believe that Roman cupidity—which saw gold purely in an economic sense, without the vital religious dimension—offended the Celts' religious feelings beyond endurance.

This argument brought us back to Boudica and the cause of the rebellion—the immense wealth of her husband, King Prasutagus. Without that, Catus would not have precipitated the rebellion. His savage treatment of Boudica and her daughters argued for a wealth so enormous that he risked disaster to get his hands on the fraction of it that would have been his due, once he had secured it for the Empire.

Gold flowed from Ireland down the course of what was to become Watling Street; and Icenian wealth—if it was so enormous—must have been based upon gold. But Watling Street led to London and Dover, and the Iceni dwelt in what is now Norfolk and north Suffolk. London was a Roman creation, which Boudica destroyed, and we had no evidence that it was connected with the gold route to continental Europe. Where did Watling Street cease to mark that route?

To answer this question we returned to High Cross, where the Fosse Way meets Watling Street. Looking east, we discerned another line across the Midland Plain. This is not marked by a Roman road but by a succession of great temples. All these temples bear the sign of trade. Beyond them, in East Anglia, we find a vast array of golden objects. This is how the gold route is marked, and its destination is the land of Iceni, of Prasutagus and his wife Boudica.

GOLDEN TEMPLES AND TORQUES

THE TRADE ROUTE from Ireland ran along the line of Watling Street from the furthermost tip of Anglesey to Mancetter. Here it moved eastward through Ratae (the modern Leicester), then the tribal center of the Coricltavi. From there it traced a line across the Midlands to East Anglia, the kingdom of the Iceni.

The route is marked by a series of important Celtic temples set within substantial trading centers: Thistleton in Leicestershire (formerly Rutland), Collyweston and Brigstock in Northamptonshire, Water Newton in Cambridgeshire, and Thetford in Norfolk. This line passes just south of the great grove of Vernemeton; some of the most spectacular finds of Celtic goldworking have been made at its eastern end. The magnificent torque (ornamental neck ring) found at Snettisham, near King's Lynn, is just one of many Celtic treasures that have been found in East Anglia. It is a small token of the Icenian wealth and, as we shall see, it is also a symbol of Lovernios's death.

Let us first look at the temples. Thistleton is close to Vernemeton and Mancetter and, unlike Vernemeton, it has been extensively excavated. A mass of Celtic relics—brooches, pottery, coins, hearths, ovens, kilns and wells—bears eloquent witness to a densely populated religious and commercial site at the time of the Roman invasion. It was situated on the boundary between the Corieltavi and the Catuvellauni (who were always in the forefront of the battle against the Romans) and clearly provided a bustling rural market, trading depot and religious center for the region.

The temple itself was discovered only through aerial photography; it was bounded by a vast ditch. A succession of temples, one above the other, was revealed, the one dating from the first century A.D. being a large wooden building. It was replaced by an imposing, limestone-clad and stone-floored edifice approached via a metaled roadway. In the third century A.D. this was replaced by an even grander basilica-style temple, reflecting the still-growing importance of the site, which had been continuously occupied since the pre-Roman period.

The temple sites at Collyweston and Brigstock in Northamptonshire, are equally extensive. Here, too, the original wooden temples were replaced by stone structures. Only at Thetford was a major temple site not overbuilt—this is one of the few original wooden Celtic temples of which the remains have been uncovered. Brigstock is well known for the large quantity of coins and bronzework unearthed in the excavations. Water Newton, on the other hand, on the edge of Icenian territory in Cambridgeshire, was an important center for pottery. The excavation revealed many pottery remains with representations of the god Mercury, who was always associated with trade in the classical world. This fact underlines a comment made by many classical authors who wrote about Celtic religions: when trying to equate the Celtic deities with their own gods and goddesses, they observed that the chief god of the Celts was Mercury.

The pagan association of Mercury with trade and traders is deeply engrained, and our analysis of the gold route and its significance in Lovernios's death pointed to a new understanding of this link with the Celts. If the Druids regulated trade through a series of substantial religious-commercial centers, Roman observers would naturally have assumed that one of their chief gods was that of trade. The Crusades provided a parallel. The twinning of religious and commercial motives behind the plundering of the Levant had allowed religious orders such as the Knights Templar to establish trading and banking systems—institutions which were the direct ancestors of those we have today.

The emerging picture of this trade route from Anglesey to East Anglia pinpointed the vital importance of the Midland section, which threaded its way between the southern edge of the Derbyshire hills and the waterlogged ground south of the Wash. We saw Mancetter as the point where the Roman road joined this route, close by the great sanctuary of Vernemeton. To Boudica and her army, the Romans were the destroyers of both ends of the trade route. If Suetonius made his stand close to the key sanctuary and trading post on the central section, the Britons had every reason to fear that the Romans threatened complete destruction of their economic wealth.

The traditional picture of the native Britons as a disorganized and primitive community of woad-painted savages, living in huts and hovels and bowing powerlessly before the Roman advance, is demolished by this uncovering of the trade route and its druidic masters. We now saw why the Romans had no need to threaten the Celts' religion, however bloodthirsty; the real target was the elite core of Druids who held the administrative, political, judicial and *economic* keys to Celtic wealth and skill.

Despite the attraction of Roman ways to the susceptible client kings in the southeast, we could see why the kingdoms that bounded and protected the gold route had no wish to be absorbed into the Empire. The Midland region was a populous area of intense native activity, and had thriving trading links with Ireland and continental Europe. Unlike the tribes of the southeast, the Celts of the interior were not used to Roman contact or to the prospect of Roman dominion, and would have been violently opposed to any imperial action that disturbed their settled ways. They were masters of a profitable and fertile terrain, organized into tribes and kingdoms united by religious beliefs and the influence of the druidic caste. The Romans posed an immense threat to them, not only to freedom of organization of daily life and trade but to the sanctified marketing and working of gold, the highest art.

We had already pinpointed the traffic in gold along this route as a religious activity. Its most vital function was producing works of art to be offered to the gods through druidic ritual. It was not difficult to guess that the Druids saw themselves as the prime victims of the Roman conquest—which would strip them of this vital economic power—and that they nevertheless had learned the lesson of Gaul and saw its inevitability. We could now see that for the Celts the worlds of commerce, craft, warfare and religion were all interwoven into a dense and inextricable whole. The world of the gods was as familiar and acceptable as the mundane activities of barter and battle, and the dazzling omni-competent Celtic Mercury— benefactor of trade, shepherd of flocks and herds, guide of souls to the otherworld—shone with a golden light over all the Celtic world.

Nowhere did he shine more brightly than in the land of the Iceni. We can catch a glimpse of Prasutagus's immense wealth from the vast and priceless array of Celtic golden objects found in East Anglia. Foremost among these are the torques.

The torque is the Celtic ornament and symbol *par excellence*. Essentially, it is a close-fitting and massy necklet, often elaborately worked or decorated in gold or other precious metal. Arguably, the finest of all Celtic torques is the one uncovered at Snettisham in 1948. This was found as part of a hilltop deposit, and the field that hid the treasure yielded five other deposits during deep plowing in the following two years. Others were later uncovered, giving a current total of sixty-one torques—by far the greatest number found on a single site in Britain. Nearly all were made of either gold or electrum (gold alloyed with a high percentage of silver). Others have been found scattered through Suffolk and Lincolnshire, and the very famous Needwood torque came to light a few miles north of Mancetter. Another golden torque was found nearby at Glascote;

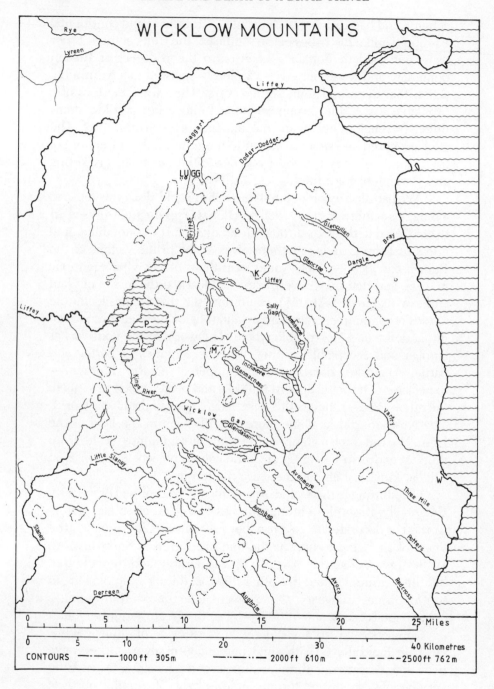

WICKLOW MOUNTAINS

and Somerset and the Scottish borders have yielded others. The most impressive, however, are the Snettisham finds.

The Snettisham deposit dates from the second half of the first century A.D., and there is every indication that the other torques were deposited at the same time. We could only presume that the treasure was buried at a time of great need and sudden disaster, and that the burial site possessed some kind of sanctity. And we could identify this disaster with Catus's depredations, the trigger for the black year.

The necklet called the Snettisham torque is unique, and has been justly called the most beautiful British antiquity. The main hoop consists of eight twisted strands, each strand made up of eight wires, culminating in massive hollow terminals cast separately, and with exquisite details.

Very few golden torques have ever been found in graves. Most seem to have been offered to the gods, although there are isolated records of torques discovered in earlier times being melted down for their precious metals. We know that the Celts reworked the precious metals into torques and there is clear evidence that the great Snettisham torque itself was made by reworking gold from melted-down objects.

Man of the Celtic deities are depicted as wearing torques, and sculptures—such as "The Dying Gaul" from Pergaman, Turkey— show this ornament. Dio Cassius described Boudica, queen and druidess, as wearing a "great twisted golden necklace" when she rode into battle. This was certainly a symbol of her authority, but it also had great totemic and religious significance. She is said to have worn it to invoke the terrible goddess Andraste after releasing the sacred hare before the final battle. Some torques, such as the massive silver and iron-cored example from Trichtingen, now in

The Wicklow Mountains. The extent of this map is indicated by an interrupted line on the map on page 108. Capital letters on this map denote the following:

C—Church Mountain, Sliabh Guth
D—Dublin, Dubh Linne
G—Glendalough
K—Kippure, 2,473 feet above Ordnance Datum
L—Lugnaquilla Mountain, 3,089 feet
M—Mullachcleevaun, 2,783 feet
P—Pollaphuca Reservoir, which incorporates a stretch of the Liffey River
W—Wicklow port

the Stuttgart Museum, were far too heavy ever to be worn, even for ceremonial use. They were clearly intended either for display on wooden images of a god or as a votive offering to be cast into a lake or pit.

Torques were the emblem of the aristocracy, of gods and goddesses, and their magic was reflected in the actions of torque-bearing divinities. This magic was not always benign, for it was often associated with enchantment and the offering of death. It is this that suddenly brings us from the eastern end of the gold route to the death of Lovernios, for when we started to look at the torque for clues to his sacrifice, we found a curious and disturbing link.

Many of the torque rings are twisted into strands, and as we examined more and more of these, we were struck by their similarity to the strands of a *noose*. Lovernios, like Tollund Man, was killed by garroting. His noose was carefully prepared from animal sinew. It could have been chicken gut, although we suggest that it was from a fox. Either way, it came from a sacred animal. The noose was doubly stranded and triply knotted with unusually short ends, cut very neatly. The similarity between garrote and torque made us wonder whether the torque could possibly have been the sacrificial weapon, the victim being either hung from it or the soft metal being twisted to break the neck. The pair of torques recovered from the sacred site of Tara reinforced our suspicion, for the open terminals bore a distinct and perhaps intended resemblance to the ends of a rope.

If Lovernios died from the twisting of the garrote, and if he was a prince or king, where was his torque? Surely he would have died wearing it, or it would have been buried with him. We knew, however, that his body, as recovered, had been naked except for the armband of fox fur. No artifact, other than a small as yet unidentified iron object, was found in the vicinity.

No torques have ever been recovered near Lindow. If we looked along the western end of the gold route, only one place presented itself as a likely votive place for such an offering. The place was on Anglesey, close by Holy Island and Caer Gybi. If Lovernios came from Ireland, as we thought, he would have made landfall close by. Here, we were sure, was the place that marked Lovernios's *via dolorosa* to Lindow. It was "the place of little stones"— Llyn Cerrig Bach.

THE LAKE OF LITTLE STONES

IN MOST ACCOUNTS of Suetonius's campaign and the Boudican rebellion, Anglesey is no more than a remote druidic stronghold, an isolated and troublesome base beyond the mountains, whose purpose was mainly to foment unrest during the Romanizing of Britain. Why should so much power lie in a tiny island like Anglesey?

We believe we have deciphered the riddle of Anglesey. Its apparent remoteness is an illusion, for it was the vital link on the gold route between the Wicklow Mountains and eastern Britain. Our understanding of Anglesey as much more than an isolated holy island of sacred groves was vital to our pinpointing of Lindow as the sacred place for the sacrifice of Lovernios and of Mancetter as the site of the final disastrous battle.

If Anglesey (Mona of the Druids) is the key to understanding the events of the black year, Llyn Cerrig Bach, the "lake of the little stones," is the key to understanding Anglesey. We saw in the previous chapter that Lovernios could only have come from Ireland and he could only have died at Lindow Moss. In Llyn Cerrig Bach, these two vital components of the black year came together.

Llyn Cerrig Bach is little known even in the archaeological world. Books on the Celts normally mention it only through an anecdote. This is powerful enough, but it gives no more than a hint of the importance of the site in explaining the reality of the gold route and the major role of Anglesey. The anecdotal evidence is this:

In 1942 the RAF started building an airfield at Valley, close by the narrows that separate the main part of Anglesey from Holy Island. During the earthmoving, which involved clearing a bog, massive iron chains were found. These were pressed into service for tractors to tow trapped trucks from the mud. Only by chance was one of them identified as Celtic metalwork. It was a massive slave chain, with six neck rings joined by heavy links, still robust enough to function for this heavy work after two thousand years.

Despite frantic efforts, made under difficult wartime conditions, only a fraction of the bog was examined for other traces of Celtic metalwork. In all, 138 objects were recovered, in whole or part. Enormous quantities of bone were found but few were retained for archaeological examination. The hurried excavation was supervised by Sir Cyril Fox, who organized the dispatching of the finds ultimately gifted to the National Museum of Wales in 1944. The site was then sealed up and further excavation rendered impossible.

Marvels of Celtic metalwork, above all of a military character, were uncovered at Llyn Cerrig Bach. Fox used the fragments of a chariot—one among some forty such vehicles identified—to reconstruct the iron-tired, wickerwork-sided Celtic fighting vehicle. This reconstruction is justly famous, but it gives the merest flavor of the riches of Llyn Cerrig Bach, which include swords, spears, daggers, shields, chariot trappings and wheels.

The deposits suggest an important sanctuary, where merchants and devotees offered sacrifices of costly weapons—and perhaps slaves as well—on landing. Fragments of bronze caldrons hint at the religious presence, which it is now clear, always underlies Celtic trade. The items so far recovered suggest that the wealth of Llyn Cerrig Bach in its entirety surpasses that of La Tène. That is not to belittle the importance of the Swiss site, for the similarities are even more important: both are lakeside offering sites, and both are on important trading routes through the Celtic world.

Nothing was found at Llyn Cerrig Bach that owed anything to Roman influence. Everything pointed to a cultural continuity through the late Iron Age which halted abruptly with the sack of Mona and the Roman presence in nearby Aberffraw soon afterward. But the links to the wider Celtic world are as strong as the links in the formidable gang chains.

The slave chain has parallels at the eastern end of the gold route, where several others, though none so formidable, have been recovered. The long and terrible spears found in the bog have close ties with the weaponry of the Celts from Leinster, in Ireland. An enduring tradition derives the name of the Lleyn peninsula, which abuts Anglesey, from the settlers who came from Leinster. If that is true, the Irish link is strengthened tenfold. Many of the chariot trappings link Llyn Cerrig Bach to what is now Devon and Somerset; others show influences from Yorkshire, the land of the Parisii, to the east of the Brigantian confederacy.

Sir Cyril Fox first identified the presence of trade and gold routes from Ireland to eastern and southwestern Britain from evidence uncovered at Llyn Cerrig Bach. That the site demonstrated intense trading activity was beyond doubt, for whatever riches Anglesey might have possessed, it is inconceivable that this tiny island could have supported an aristocratic population wealthy enough to have made all these offerings. We believe that it was a depot and trading center.

The Roman evidence shows that it was certainly a druidic stronghold, and it is tempting to see Suetonius's view that the island was a granary of the resistance as reflecting a gross underestimation of its true wealth. It was a major trading center controlled by the Druids.

Our identification of the black year as the time of Lovernios's death inevitably linked him to Anglesey, but his unblemished state argued against him being a survivor of the Roman massacre, or of the druidic rearguard that fled with Caratacus into the Welsh hills.

Instead, we at first favored the view that he came from Ireland at the time of disaster, but arrived too late to participate in the ritual cursing on the shores of the Menai Straits because of the encircling

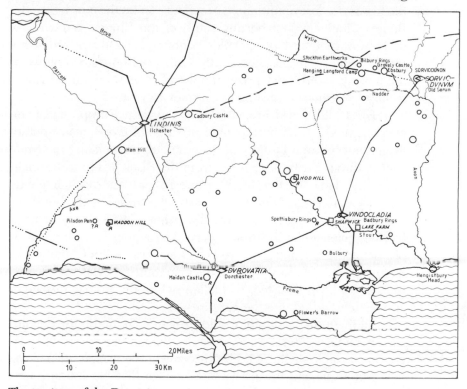

The territory of the Durotriges.

Roman navy. In the immediate aftermath of Suetonius's headlong flight to save Roman Britain from Boudica, Lovernios landed on Anglesey and saw the ruins of the sacred groves. Then he heard the report of the disaster that had overwhelmed Boudica at Mancetter. Thus he learned of the destruction of druidism.

How black was the Celtic night to become? And how to stave off its uttermost darkness? It was Lovernios's arrival that provided the key.

HALTING THE ROMAN ADVANCE

LET US TRY and see that bleak and nightmarish picture of a collapsing world for a moment through Lovernios's eyes. Britain south of the Dee was in Roman hands. North of the Mersey was the client kingdom of Brigantia, fatally enmeshed in the toils of Roman intrigue. Eastward, the gold route was wholly lost and the wealth of the Iceni gone forever into Roman coffers. Across the North Sea, the Roman frontier was stabilizing south of the Rhine. In Denmark there was another type of gold—amber—a highly prized jewel sought avidly by the classical south. Only the Rhine stood between the Romans and this rich prize, and with Britain subdued, what was to stop the legions returning to conquer Germany?

The Celtic world in central and southern Europe had been overwhelmed by the unstoppable progress of the Roman military juggernaut. Once a Druid had been able to travel *along the trade routes*, through tribe after tribe, from the Black Sea to Ireland and from the Baltic to the Mediterranean, passing through Celtic territory all the way. Now it was nearly all eclipsed by the burgeoning Roman Empire. In the east, the richness marked by La Tène had long fallen under the Roman yoke. The famous Hochdorf burial, of a richly dressed and accoutred chieftain swathed in Chinese silk, hints at an eastern counterpart of the gold route that we now know as the silk road. All this, too, had fallen before the Roman onslaught and been absorbed into the Empire.

All that remained, and would ever remain, and *must* remain, was Ireland, the *insula sacra*. And the Roman presence on Mona, the unstoppable might of their arms, made the narrow strip of sea between Mona and the Irish coast look, in that bleak hour, a far weaker barrier than the Rhine.

What was to stop the Romans invading Ireland? Druidic curses had not stayed them at the Menai Straits. Boudica had been trapped into a hopeless defeat at Mancetter; the economic power of the Druids was broken.

Now we see why he chose, and was chosen, to die. His sacrifice was offered not only to placate the gods but to stave off the Roman threat to Ireland. He died naked, with the fox fur armband as the only token of kingly rank, as subtly marked as Christ, who had died in torment a generation before. But a symbol, Lovernios's "crown of thorns," was missing. What of his torque, the ultimate symbol of the fusion of king and Druid?

Lovernios, we suggest, made his somber landfall on the coast of Mona, close by the lake of little stones where, under the watchful eyes of the Druids, rich offerings were made for the gods of trade. When Lovernios arrived with his retinue of Druids, we have already surmised that he was too late to work any magic on the Romans and that the customary sacrifices were of no avail. The groves were felled, the Druids were struck down. Detachments of legionnaires undoubtedly held the island and the line of Watling Street, while the main force sought the decisive battle with Boudica. The sea was Roman too, for Suetonius's navy cruised around the coast.

There was nothing for Lovernios in Anglesey. Its sanctity was destroyed; it was no place for the supreme sacrifice. Instead, the waters of Llyn Cerrig Bach were fit only to receive his symbols of kingship. Somewhere here, perhaps beneath the wartime runway, may lie his massive torque, woven with gold wires into the pattern of the sacred noose. It was a symbol, no more, like a horseshoe at the doorway, keeping evil out. Llyn Cerrig Bach was the place for the symbol, not the sacrifice.

Lovernios departed from the sacred lake in sorrow and stealth, probably by night and, we believe, by sea. The Roman presence dictated that the strange forgotten corner of Cornovia, Lindow, would be his final resting place. It was indeed the death of Lovernios that made Lindow sacred, that made this obscure corner of Britain—and later England—a fierce and enduring Celtic enclave. We see now why it retained its legend of the king in the ground, and the Druid in the cave, and the white horse beyond price, as a marker against the day of his discovery and the unraveling of the golden thread of his somber story.

Despite their navy and despite the consolidation of their grip on Britain in the decades that followed Lovernios's death, the Romans never did go to Ireland, and never went beyond the Rhine.

RECESSIONAL

WHAT, THEN, was the eventual outcome of Lindow Man's violent death? What happened to his passionate belief in a happy ending, and enduring existence, and a timely resuscitation?

We believe that his death has justified itself to a greater extent than he himself—at that time of terror, despair, and threatened destruction of his holy order—could have hoped. His death and his sudden reappearance some two thousand years later have focused the eyes and imagination of the world upon his life and times. The Celts and the European Iron Age have come to the forefront of academic interest and research. And the Druids, a long discredited topic, are once again a subject for serious study and discussion. If it should turn out that our deductions about Lindow Man's life and death add to this, then Lindow Man will have gained more than his intended objective.

The wider region of Lindow Moss, and central England in general, still celebrates the old festivals, and acknowledges the ancient forces that lurk in the folk-memory, as we have seen. Here, in the heartland of England, and at the end of the twentieth century, in spite of all our technological progress, man still experiences the deep, subconscious need to *avoid*, to *acknowledge*, and to *devote*.

What can strange survivals such as the Haxey hood game, sword dancing with ritual "decapitation," and well-dressings be but the remnants of ancient druidism, satisfying some dormant need for purification and propitiation by means of bloodletting and offering hope of renewal and rebirth?

THE PRIESTESS IN THE MOSS?

LINDOW MOSS may have been a place of superstitious dread for a long time, perhaps even before the special sacrifice which imbued it with strange, dark sanctity in the black year.

Is there any evidence for other sacrificial offerings to the moss? The head of Lindow Woman, found in May 1983, some 250 yards from where the Druid prince still lay entombed in the peat, has recently been dated to the second century A.D. by radiocarbon methods. Could a female head have been "offered" to this extraordinary peat bog at that point?

Little more than twenty years after the death of Lovernios, England and Wales were firmly under Rome's control and Agricola was advancing to the Forth–Clyde line. In A.D. 84 he defeated the Caledonian tribes at Mons Craupius. But Scotland was never truly pacified. An insurrection was suppressed in A.D. 118, and in A.D. 122 Hadrian commissioned the Tyne–Solway Wall. Trouble from the northern tribes continued and in A.D. 139–142, the Romans advanced north again to build the Antonine Wall from the Forth to the Clyde, along the line fortified previously by Agricola. But the wall was evacuated between A.D. 161 and 165, and thirty years later the north was ablaze again.

Hadrian's Wall was attacked by the Maeatae, joined by the Picts, Scotti, and others. Finding forts virtually deserted, the northern tribesmen threw down the gateways and the walls, and (significantly) decapitated statues as they swarmed southward. They continued as far as York and Chester, pillaging and burning as they went.

The Celtic holy places had never been forgotten. Stories of the supreme sacrifice would still have been current in the countryside around Lindow Moss. It had happened at a dark place in dark times, but when freedom from oppression was still a possibility. Now, well over a century later, British tribes, scenting freedom yet again, converged on the borders of Lindow Moss, on their way to Chester (Deva), the legionary fortress at the head of the Dee Estuary.

Did they turn aside and make another sacrificial offering to the powers of Lindow Moss in the form of the female head, severed from some priestess in their midst? Who was she, this woman of some thirty years (a significant druidic age)—a druidess, a princess, a cherished captive? And where does her body lie? Lindow Moss still keeps its secrets.

THE TRIPLE ECHO

LINDOW MOSS is a strange place. Even now the rugged rocks and rocky moors that enfold the wasteland are haunted by strange forces and sinister manifestations. Memories of the ancient gods still disturb the minds of those whose paths lie in the depths of this lonely landscape. Those who live on the edge of Lindow still warn their children to beware of its water spirits, its treacherous pools and boggy hollows. Was it always so? Was Lindow Moss the destined resting place for sacrificial victims in remote times before Lindow Man met his end there?

In the winter of 1987, a second naked body was extracted from the same area of the Cheshire peat bog. It was in fragmentary condition, but the elegance of the surviving hand again indicated elevated social status. The evidence pointed to sacrificial death. Scientists and forensic experts have been working steadily on the assembled remains, and although the picture is not yet complete, some details have emerged. The body proved to be that of an adult male, aged about twenty-five. The head of Lindow Man II, which was not recovered, may have rested close to the body. Or it may have been offered separately to some potent deity in a different area of the Moss.

As in the case of Lovernios, the vertebrae show evidence of some osteoarthritis. Of special interest is the presence of an extra, undeveloped digit immediately below the thumb. That alone would have given rise to superstitious surmise, and would have marked the man out from infancy as special. Deities depicted on Gallo-Roman

128

altars sometimes have an extra finger on a splayed hand, and Celtic customs and beliefs connected with the hand are legion. Did the young man's singular hand mark him out for early druidic training?

A large piece of the gut was recovered from the peat, and it contained more food than that of Lovernios. Analysis is still in progress, and the results are eagerly awaited. Will there be traces of a blackened pancake again? Sometimes there were as many as three sacrifices at Beltain assemblies. Will there be evidence of mistletoe having once more played some part in the ceremony? Perhaps there will be traces of an alcoholic beverage consumed with the last ritual meal.

But the story of Lovernios is not yet complete. On June 14, 1988, a left knee and a large piece of skin were found in the Moss, and it is believed that these belong to his body. The skin makes up half of the right buttock, the whole of the left buttock and the anus, with possibly some pubic hair. There is no evidence of the genitals. In September 1988, a fragment of a thigh was recovered. On this evidence, it seems likely that Lovernios's body was complete when it was consigned to the pool, apart, perhaps, from the genitalia. These might have been removed at some stage during the sacrificial act, probably after the final *coup de grâce* was administered. We are unlikely ever to know for certain. At no point in their history do the Celts seem to have been interested in erotica. Celtic art and the vernacular tradition alike are singularly devoid of this genre, which was prevalent in the Roman world. The genitalia of both sexes were undoubtedly associated with fertility; but it would seem that their link with the supernatural and their widely revered power to avert evil was the basis of their major role in Celtic art, ritual and folklore. Assuming, therefore, that at some stage in the dramatic death rites Lovernios was in fact emasculated, the organs may well have been offered to the goddess of the terrain, Anu of Brigantia or Arnemetia, a water goddess.

Lindow Moss guards its dark secrets closely. But those we have been able to share testify amply to the truth of much ancient tradition.

We have indeed looked on Avalon, and glimpsed the dark interior of the pagan Celtic otherworld.

THE DRUIDS

THE CELTIC WORLD, past and present, appears as an amalgam of people sharing languages and cultural traditions, but apparently having no common ethnic origin. When they first attracted the attention of classical commentators—about 600 B.C.—the Celts were already distinctive and widespread. They knew themselves as a nation, or nations, and they were bound together as such, in spite of geographical and climatic divergencies, and in spite of endless internecine conflicts.

How was this unity possible? Was there some ultimate central government that dictated policy and controlled the heterogeneous tribal hierarchies? The answer must be "no." Each tribe had its own king or chieftain (or, toward the end of the free Celtic period, its magistrate or pair of magistrates), but there was no "Celtic" ruler, no Celtic empire. How, then, did this remarkable homogeneity arise? Who controlled it, and how was its continuity ensured?

THREEFOLD WAY

THE ANSWERS to these questions provide us with the key to the nature of the early Celtic world. The unity of Celtic society and its ultimate control rested with the "men of art," the triumvirate of learned men headed everywhere by the Druids, who were more than priests. They were statesmen who controlled the warriors and through them the tribes. In their hands lay the secrets of the Celtic soul, its fate in the past and in the future, in this life and the next.

The names of this threefold class are recorded both by the classics
and by the Celts themselves. In Gaul they were *Druids, Vates* and
Bards; the Irish equivalents were *Druidh, Filidh* and *Bard.* Both
the wide lands of Gaul and the small area of Britain or the Pretannic
Isles knew this threefold division.

The Druids had an intertribal, indeed pan-tribal, power and
authority, but they were not omnipotent. Bards and Vates also had
religious offices to perform and the Vates seem to have carried out
the sacrifices at which Druids had to be present, for no sacrifice

The Celtic attachment to the number three is attested in countless material and
literary themes. Nowhere is this feeling more elegantly displayed than in this
example of the triskele—an openwork bronze ornament, with three holes for
attachment in the rim, from CARNVNTVM, PANNONIA, a Roman military base and
seat of government twenty miles east of Vienna on the right bank of the Danube
River.

could be conducted without the sanction and authority of a presiding priest. Classical comments on the Druids are often described as secondhand, as based on "value judgment" or as political propaganda (denigrating the enemy to show the superiority of the opposition, usually Roman). But we believe that reports of early observation must be re-examined in the light of recent archaeological evidence, and our analysis of Lindow Man.

The testimony of Julius Caesar is of the first importance, for Caesar was not merely a soldier and statesman but a priest of the Roman state cult, much concerned with religious matters. He was therefore interested in druidism and in understanding its importance in Celtic society. Moreover, he was a friend of a pro-Roman Druid—Diviciacus—and knowledgeable about Druid beliefs, especially those concerned with the gods and with life after death. Caesar points out in the *Gallic War* that the Gauls treated their common folk almost as slaves. The two classes who mattered were the Druids and the knights. The Druids were concerned with divine worship, the due performance of sacrifices public and private, the interpretation of ritual questions, settlement of disputes and the punishment of those who refused to accept their ruling. Caesar asserts that Druid power originated in Britain and that Britain remained the center of druidism.

The Druids taught their acolytes the druidical secrets by word of mouth. They chanted the lessons to their students, who sang them back to their masters until they knew them by heart. In their judicial function of settling disputes, the Druids determined the amount of damages due to the wronged parties. Their role in determining succession was crucial, as the early vernacular tradition of Ireland makes clear. There were constant boundary disputes requiring druidic intervention. In Gaul, those who disobeyed druidic decisions were banished from the tribe or the wider community, and there are hints in Caesar's writings that they were in danger of becoming sacrificial victims, fuel for the Beltain fires.

THE DRUIDIC INSTITUTION

IRELAND WAS NEVER conquered by the Romans. It is therefore the ideal place in which to study the Druids. Evidence suggests that druidism in Ireland was similar to that in Britain and Gaul, and probably in the entire Celtic world. Intertribal assemblies took place at several sites, the main ones being "sanctified" places, where people from the whole island gathered. We may be sure that the same applied to Britain. The assemblies took no account of tribal boundaries; they concerned the whole country. Ireland was divided into five districts or communities, independent of one another, but unified by the great national feasts and gatherings. Here the Druids played their essential part. It was druidism rather than any other ethnic or historical factor that bonded the miscellaneous Celtic peoples into a distinctive and enduring whole.

The chief centers in Ireland for the gatherings were at Carman, on the plain called the Curragh of Kildare; in Uisnech, in modern Westmeath—a site believed to be the center of the country—and at Taltiu, Tlachtga and Tara, all close to one another in County Meath. The assemblies took place on days vital to the agricultural year: *Beltain*, May 1, the beginning of summer; *Lughnasa*, August 1, the beginning of autumn; and *Samain*, November 1, the beginning of winter. The Uisnech assemblies were held at Beltain, the Taltiu and Carman festivals at Lughnasa and the Tlachtga and Tara gatherings at Samain. Some of the assemblies were annual, others triennial. The triennial ones are likely to have been of particular splendor.

Both continental and Irish Druids claimed superiority to kings, unless they themselves held both offices. They called themselves "creators of the universe," a title that indicates their high self-esteem. They clearly saw themselves as gods incarnate. In Ireland, kings went nowhere without their Druids. As in Ireland, so in Britain, there must have been holy sites, places of periodic national assembly. Mon (Anglesey)—the sanctuary destroyed by the Romans in A.D. 60—may have been a place where both Irish and British Druids convened assemblies.

There is much evidence to substantiate Caesar's claim that the origins of druidism lay in the British Isles. Ireland was known to the classical writers as *insula sacra*, the sacred island, and there druidism continued as a functioning religion until the coming of Christianity put an official "end" to this ancient pagan belief. In Britain, native priests would have supervised the native cults acceptable to the Empire, and druidism itself would have survived in some form in remote districts: in Midland glades, in the mountains of Wales and Cumbria, in the Scottish Highlands and in the demon-haunted Western Isles of ancient Irish tradition.

SACRED GROVES AND ISLANDS

THE CELTS seem to have regarded islands as especially sacred places. Mona was clearly an island of considerable holiness. The Isle of Man, sacred to the sea god, Manannan, appears to have possessed similar sanctity. A stone slab found there in the last century bears an inscription in Celtic Ogam script that translates: "The Stone of Dovaidona, son of the Druid." This implies that there were Druids on Man as late as the fifth or sixth century. And it seems likely that the sacred status of many small islands in pagan times continued with the coming of Christianity. The fact that the three sons of the fifth-century northern Irish king Erc were buried on Iona seems to suggest that there was a royal (and pagan) cemetery on the island before the coming of Columba. Oran, one of Columba's brethren, seems to have been sacrificed when the foundations of the monastery were laid. Perhaps it was to propitiate the pagan spirits that still inhabited the island.

Welsh legend has it that a similar sacrifice was recommended by the Druids during the building of Vortigern's castle. No progress was made because the stones disappeared as soon as they were laid. The Druids ordered that a child, born without a father, should be sacrificed and its blood sprinkled over the site to cleanse it. Pliny records that the slaying of a human being was a highly religious act among the Britons, and the eating of the flesh regarded as a "wholesome remedy." The Roman historian Diodorus Siculus states that the Irish ate their enemies, and the Greek historian and traveler Pausaniaus tells how the Galatian Celts ate the flesh and drank the blood of children. Solinus describes the Irish tradition of washing the face in the blood of the slain, and imbibing it. The blood of dead relatives was also drunk by the Irish and this custom persisted into the sixteenth century. Blood brotherhood survived into comparatively recent times in areas such as the Western Isles. All these were clearly ritual acts, and certainly point to druidic influence.

In considering Caesar's suggestion that druidism had British origins, we must remember the impressive prehistoric monuments which are clearly of a ceremonial and ritual nature and imply a *national* rather than a *tribal* concern. The possibility that they are linked to the Druids can no longer be lightly dismissed, although for many years no serious scholar would discuss it. The subject had been brought into disrepute by the intense antiquarian preoccupation with Stonehenge and pseudo-druidic activities there and elsewhere. We do not need to join those who assert that the Druids *built* Stonehenge; we simply observe that they may have *used* it. There is certainly ample evidence that the Druids used Stone Age burial chambers and stone circles for their rites in Ireland.

It seems likely that such sites as Pilsdon Pen in Dorset, Navan Fort Emain Macha in County Armagh and the numerous "hostelries" (*bruiden*) mentioned in the early Irish literature, provided accommodation for the many students of druidism in Celtic countries. These are perhaps forerunners of the numerous and well-attested schools of Dark Age Ireland that provided free board, lodging and textbooks to refugee scholars from Europe and Britain after the sack of Rome by the Visigoth Alaric in A.D. 410.

The Druids were exempt from military service and did not pay war taxes. These privileges, according to Caesar, attracted many young men to the schools of druidism, where for up to twenty years they learned verses by heart. The Druids reserved writing for private and public accounts and business. This, Caesar says, was to keep the verses secret and to cultivate the memory.

DRUIDIC BELIEFS

DOCTRINALLY, CAESAR SAYS the most important Druid belief was that after death the soul passes from one to another—hence the Celts' bravery in battle. There is indeed strong evidence that the Celts believed not only in continued existence beyond the tomb, but in rebirth in both human and animal form. Involved and fantastical tales of such transformations are characteristic of Celtic mythology. For example, the magical bulls in the Irish prose epic *Táin Bó Cúailnge*, "The Cattle Raid of Cooley," were possessed of human reason, having originated as two swineherds of the Lord of the Otherworld. They then passed through a long series of metamorphoses—becoming ravens, stags, warriors, water monsters, demons and aquatic worms. It can hardly be doubted that the myth of the Brown Bull (or Lordly Bull) of Cuailnge is closely related to (and perhaps identical to) the Tarvos Trigaranus of Gaulish tradition. Nor is it really in question that the slaying of the mythic bull depicted on the basal plate of the Gundestrup caldron, which we considered in more detail in Chapter 5 for its druidical significance, is another reflection of the divine Celtic bull hunt.

All the disciplines—archaeology, the classics, and the vernacular tradition down to the present day—reinforce Caesar's assertion. The lavish grave goods, the equipment for the journey and for the Otherworld feast that awaited the traveler beyond the tomb, the

Esus felling a tree, one panel of a pair of four-sided blocks, probably originally parts of an altar, found during excavations in the choir of Nôtre Dame church, Paris, France, in 1711.

choice festal food, including joints of pork and great caldrons of heady mead and ale, convey an unequivocal message.

The Celts had no fear of death. This was not due to carelessness of life, nor to reckless bravado; it arose from deep and ancient inherited beliefs, taught by the Druids through countless generations. Recitation of ancestry, the cult of graves (many of the seasonal assemblies were held at burial places, including the enigmatic

TARVOS TRIGARANVS, the bull with three cranes, which features on another panel; the remaining panels feature JOVIS and VOLCANVS.

passage graves that stud Ireland), the belief in the interweaving of the spiritual and mundane worlds so that the two could hardly be separated—these are all ancient Celtic and proto-Celtic attitudes and point clearly to the essential and archaic nature of druidism.

The future life was envisaged as an extension of earthly existence, where all the pleasures of this world were present, but intensified; where even fighting was permitted (though the warriors lived to fight another battle), where the slaughtered festive pig was alive and awaiting the same fate on the following day. It was a place to which mortals could go, and from whence immortals could reenter the realms of the living.

Irish and Welsh traditions refer constantly to the druidic concept of a happy Otherworld, a land (or island) of perpetual youth and constant delight. All these pleasures possibly referred to the privileged classes alone; the common people were of little account in the tradition. Heroes are sired by gods. In one version of his legend, the Ulster king Conchobar was the reincarnation of a river god, his mother having swallowed two worms in a draft of water from the river. The mother of the hero Conall Cernach was barren until a Druid chanted spells over a well in which she bathed.

The incantations of the Druids, assisted by the addition of mistletoe to the waters, bring forth life. These beliefs are attested in the sacrifice of the young Druid at Lindow Moss—the life-giving powers of the pool, the magic mistletoe with its procreative pollen, and the spells and incantations of the officiating Druids—all ensuring perpetual life for the dying man to the greater glory of his people.

DRUIDIC KNOWLEDGE AND POWER

CAESAR CLAIMS for the Druids a knowledge of astronomy, intermixed with astrology. The Coligny calendar certainly reveals a knowledge of astronomy, and other sources, too, indicate that Caesar's comment is well founded. The Druids claimed to have created the universe, and taught that the world was indestructible, but that both fire and water would at some time prevail. The souls of men were, like the world, held to be permanent. And the soul was clothed in a body in the Otherworld. Druidic doctrine was a closely guarded secret. It was difficult for the Greeks and Romans fully to

Extract of two of the sixty months shown on the Coligny calendar (pages 150–51) and section through the calendar.

comprehend such fragments of the dogma as were available to them, and even harder for them to regard these fragments objectively. So it is all the more remarkable that the classical record corresponds so closely to that of archaeology.

All sources testify to Caesar's statement that the Gauls (otherwise Celts) were devoted to religion. They also support what he says about their predilection for human sacrifice. Sacrifices could be both on a private or grander public level. The Celts believed in capital punishment, but they turned it into a religious act, making an execution into a sacrifice. Innocents were sacrificed too, and after a defeat, a great leader would offer himself. The Celts would on occasion turn their weapons against themselves and, by self-sacrifice, attempt to redeem their threatened fellows. Sacrifices were made to bring about victory, and when victory was secured, by way of thanksgiving to the gods. Captives were vowed to the gods before battle, and for this reason could not be sold or given away. They had to be offered. Human beings were sacrificed in order to propitiate the god of blight and crop failure.

Evil deeds by individuals, kings in particular, could bring disease and retard growth. In one Irish tale the Druids proclaimed that the only cure was to sacrifice the son of an undefiled couple, and to sprinkle his blood upon the doorposts and upon the earth. In the *Dindschenchas*—"stories about prominent places"—which come down to us in written form from the twelfth century, human sacrifices were recorded as being offered to Crom Gruaich. Innocent victims were also offered as foundation sacrifices. A human victim was sacrificed to the foundations of the great sacred dwelling or sanctuary at Emain Macha.

THE MEN OF ART

ANCESTOR WORSHIP by the Celts, and the cult of the dead, are amply attested. Even in modern times, archaeology has been seriously handicapped in Celtic regions because of a superstitious dislike of interference with places of the dead, occasioning violent hostility in some instances. This has, in many ways, been a blessing in disguise, preserving valuable sites from amateur excavation. Irish kings were inaugurated frequently on the sites of ancestral burials, and passage graves in Ireland were closely associated with the deities.

In Ireland, the great festivals were held in honor of a dead ancestor or deity and took place at the burial site. The Eve of Samain was the great time for commemorating the dead, but they were also remembered at Lughnasa, the festival of fertility.

Certain sacrificed persons represented the spirits of fertility, and there is a hint of this in the presence of the mistletoe in Lindow Man's last meal or drink, fertility here being synonymous with the well-being of the people. On the Eve of Samain it was customary throughout the Celtic world to put food out for the dead, who walked at that time, entered the dwellings and sat at the hearths. This custom continued down to the present century. The dead were not regarded as benign, but frequently held to be tricksters and to possess potent powers of evil like the fairies, who were themselves sometimes regarded as the dead.

Sucellos, a Celtic equivalent of the Roman father god Dis, testifies, by the widespread and fundamental nature of his cult, to the truth of Caesar's statement as to the Celtic belief in descent from a divine ancestor, a *credo* taught and perpetuated by the Druids themselves.

Druidism must have been well established and known by the fourth century B.C. or earlier, for the Druids arc mentioned by Aristotle. The origins of druidism are obscure, but many clues point to the complexity and philosophical nature of druidic doctrines. The habit of *thought* and a tendency to favor intellectual rather than worldly pursuits still characterize the Celtic attitude to life. Diogenes Laertius, who lived in the third century A.D. and wrote a compendium on the lives of the philosophers, comments that philosophy was widely held to be an invention of the barbarians. The Indian Gymnosophists and Druids "make their pronouncements by means of riddles and dark sayings, teaching that the gods must be worshiped, and no evil done, and manly behavior maintained."

These values—attention to proper worship, avoidance of wickedness, and fair play—are those upheld by the medieval Christian chivalric code. And the early vernacular tradition supports this in striking detail. As the teaching of the sacred lore was by word of mouth, mnemonics played an important role in assisting students to memorize enormous quantities of material and, in due course, to

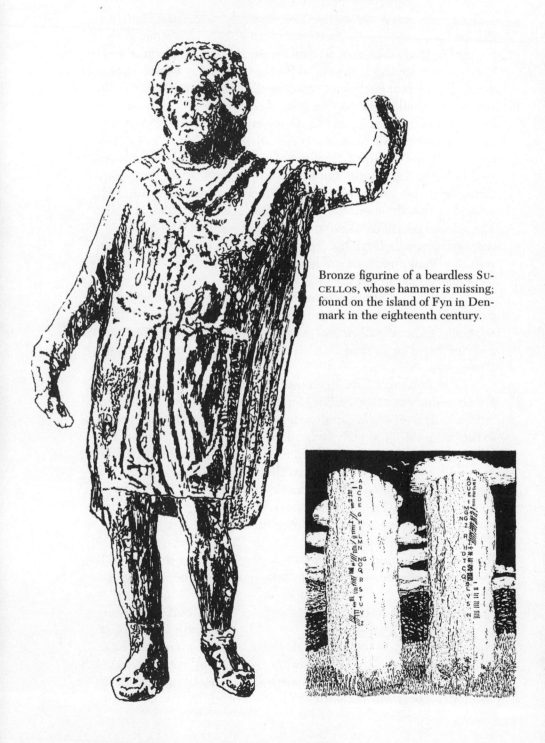

Bronze figurine of a beardless Su-
CELLOS, whose hammer is missing;
found on the island of Fyn in Denmark in the eighteenth century.

pass it on to new students. Poetic meter and complex rhyme, so characteristic of the early bardic poetry, were as important as the classification of historical and probably religious material into triads. The triadic formulae were, of course, more likely to remain in the memory. The Druids did use writing for mundane matters, Greek letters at first and later Roman. Ogam, a cryptic writing, was used in the main for commemorative inscriptions on wood and stone.

The basis of Celtic society is demonstrably based on ancient and holy tradition, and there can be no doubt that this is suffused with the precepts of druidism. The question of "manly behavior" arises time after time in the earliest traditions of Ireland; the custom of single combat is one frequent example. The evidence suggests that, originally, "men of special gifts" such as Druids, seers, bards, and that semi-religious class of intellectual poets, the *fili* who took over part of the druidic role in the early Christian period, had the freedom to pass without hindrance through tribal boundaries. This again reflects the national, rather than regional, character of the learned classes. A reverence for learning and academic titles, as well as for the "cloth" is still prevalent in modern Celtic societies.

From the comments made by the Druid Diviciacus, known

The twenty letters of the Ogam alphabet normally take the form of grooves cut into wood or stone, stemming from either a natural angle of the stone or from a drawn line, the stemline. The name "Ogam" derives from the Celtic god Ogma (Ireland) or Ogmios (Gaul), the god of eloquence. The alphabet was probably developed for the Irish language in the first instance, in immediately pre-Christian times (fifth century A.D.) and based on the Latin alphabet.

The Ogam letters were each known by the name of a tree—B, *betha*, birch; C, *coll*, holly; D, *daur*, oak; and so on. The vowels in almost all the Ogam inscriptions found in Ireland, Wales, and southern England are formed by short notches—one notch for A, two for O, three for U, four for E, and five for I. Inscriptions from the Isle of Man and much of Scotland exhibit a longer groove rather than a notch for a vowel. Whether a notch or a short line, however, the vowel is placed on the angle of the stone or on the stemline, as are the oblique lines representing the five consonants, M, G, NG, Z, and R. In the other two categories of five sounds each, the consonants B, L, V, S, and N appear on one side of the stem, while H, D, T, C, and Q appear on the other. An Ogam inscription will follow the angle of a stone up and over the top and down the other side if the length of the inscription warrants such an extension.

In the illustration, the Ogams on the stone to the left are in alphabetical order; those on the other stone are in design categories—the notches of the vowels above the three groups of five consonants.

personally by Caesar, it is clear that the part the order played in the
administrative life of the Gaulish people included divination and
augury. With the coming of the Romans to Gaul, however, the
national assembly (or assemblies) could no longer meet. This led to
the disruption of corporate druidism, and the end of the *political*
significance of the order. But that is not to say that Druids did not
continue as priests of the Celtic deities, as interpreted by Rome.

Around 8 B.C., long after Gaul had been Romanized, Diodorus
Siculus wrote that the Gaulish soothsayers foretold the future by
stabbing a man above the midriff and observing the convulsions of
his limbs and the pouring of his blood. No one performed a sacrifice
without the guidance of a philosopher, for it was held that offerings
to the gods ought only to be made through the mediation of men
learned in the divine nature. It was not only in peacetime, Diodorus

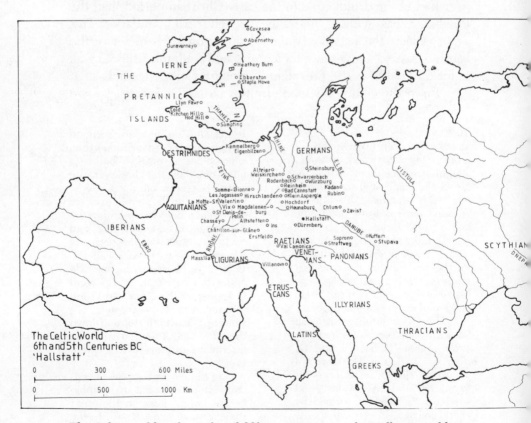

The Celtic world in the sixth and fifth centuries B.C.—the Hallstatt world—as
indicated by a selection of names of find-spots.

reported, but in war also, that the seers enjoyed authority. "Often, when the combatants are ranged face to face . . . these men come between the armies and stay the battle, just as wild beasts are sometimes held spellbound." The truth of Diodorus's observations is confirmed by insular sources. The Druids did not normally act as combatants, but they were deeply involved in combat, as magicians, as prophets, as advisers, and as intercessors with the gods.

Using elaborate spells and prayers, Druids frequently affected the outcome of battle. Rites had to be correctly performed; a wrong chant or incantation was believed to bring about disastrous results. Dancing, too, was employed as a kind of magic. The Druids circumambulated the armies of Ireland on one foot, "using one arm and one eye" (a ritual posture), and chanting to ward off the powers of the opponents. Such exercises would have involved considerable strain on the muscles of the back, as would constant prayer with the arms upraised, and might explain the early form of osteoarthritis found in the spine of Lindow Man.

The Druids were thought to have great powers over the elements, and seem to have practiced hypnotism. Such powers are acknowledged even in the Christian lives of the saints—which are a rich source of druidic lore. They could send showers of fire onto opposing hosts, and induce magical sleep, as could the harpists; the Druid Mathgen ("Born of a Bear") claimed that he could throw mountains at the enemy, and the Druids could allegedly transform trees or stones into armed men to confuse and intimidate enemies.

The power wielded by the Druids extended far beyond the practice of their religion, as we can see from the Roman proscription. For the Romans proscribed the *priesthood,* not the religion itself, which persisted and was even substantially Romanized during the period of Roman rule in Britain. Numerous shrines and dedications provide ample evidence of this. Yet the Romans were generally tolerant of "barbarian" religions, paying them serious official attention only if their tenets clashed with mandatory worship of the Emperor. Such conflict was unlikely to occur with any of the polytheistic religions because they could always accommodate another god without much difficulty.

Monotheistic religions, such as Judaism and Christianity, on the other hand, found themselves on a collision course with Rome when their adherents came within the Empire, for the denial of the godhead of the Emperor was tantamount to treason against the state. This is why the pagan religion of the British Celts survived proscription, was institutionalized and brought out of the druidic groves and into Roman-style temples. A priesthood was appointed for the important Celtic deities and for the worship of the Emperor, but its wings were clipped. The political power of the Druids had been destroyed.

A priesthood exercising temporal power outside its religious base is nothing new. The history of Christian Europe is full of examples of religious leaders who have exercised a powerful influence on politics, and today we see similar political roles played by religious leaders in theocratic states based on Islamic fundamentalism. Druidism differed essentially from these examples in that it was a cultural rather than a nationalistic force, spread across all the Celtic realms, whether they were inside or outside the Roman Empire. It was an integral part of the Celtic identity, and to understand how it arose we have to trace it back to its deepest Celtic roots.

The upper part of a figure, probably a Druid, featured on a relief forming part of an altar or a funerary monument, found in OROLANVM, now Arlon, Luxembourg.

Bear, with what has been recognized as the head of a goat between its front paws, carved on a piece of Indian sardonyx; found at the Romano-British administrative center ARBEIA, South Shields, County Durham (Tyne and Wear), England.

IRELAND AND THE DRUIDS

THE DRUIDIC PRACTICE of human sacrifice was banned by Rome in Gaul in the first century A.D., although simulated human sacrifice, and animal sacrifice, were permissible. Though druidic schools were abolished, Druids probably continued to be the natural choice as teachers in the Roman schools that replaced them. In Ireland, the druidic schools survived until the advent of Christianity, and it is clear that the academic excellence of the pagan priest-philosophers was likewise channeled into the new schools of the Celtic Church. It is useful to consider ways in which druidism manifested itself in Ireland and how the Celts themselves regarded their druidic heritage.

Gaelic seems to be the older branch of the Celtic languages; if the Druids were an integral feature of archaic Celtic society, the Gaelic dialects might be expected to reflect that. And they do. At some stage in its history Celtic society must have known a long period of stability, a space of time long enough for a language to have evolved based on ideas and concepts rather than simply on actions and objects. The complexity and subtlety of the Gaelic language is such that it clearly evolved around the needs of an educated elite rather than those of men whose lives centered on physical action and mundane preoccupations. The Gaelic language is one of the most difficult tongues in the world. And it is in its linguistic complexities and subtleties, rather than in its material remains, that Ireland stores the secrets of its druidic past, the lost system of philosophy and beliefs that was likened more than once by classical observers to that of Pythagoras. Even today, the scholar, the priest and the poet still command high respect in Gaelic society.

It is generally held that the form of Celtic (Q Celtic) spoken in Ireland, Scotland and until recently in the Isle of Man, is closer to the original form, which at some stage split up into two dialects, the P form being spoken in Gaul and Britain. British Druids would have used a form of P Celtic in their daily dealings but the archaic Q forms may have survived in their priestly functions, which were secret from the laity.

The fact that verses were used for the handing on of tradition (the Irish and Welsh triadic forms were a mnemonic aid) explains the persisting sense of sanctity with which poetry is imbued in the Celtic world. The metrical complexity of Old Irish rhyming and the later bardic poetic meter systems probably sprang from the druidic oral tradition. Mathematical calculations, cosmology and astronomy could all be communicated and learned through the spoken word. So much that appears incomprehensible in the early Irish language becomes meaningful when it is envisaged against a sophisticated background of philosophical and scientific discipline. Although the point cannot be conclusively proved, the cumulative evidence indicates that the Q Celtic languages are extremely ancient. We may also note that many of the traces of Q Celtic in Europe have to do with names of divinities—for example, Ucuetis, Sequana, Sinquatis, Quariatis.

The Gaulish Druids came to Britain to perfect their arts and it may well be that Wales, with its druidic stronghold on Mona (Anglesey), was the center for these advanced druidic studies, using perhaps a special hieratic language to communicate the mysteries. The central role of Mona emerges strongly in our final analysis of Lindow Man's death.

Gold lozenge-shaped plaque found with other objects of gold in the burial under Bush Barrow at Normanton Down, near Amesbury, Wiltshire, England.

THE BUSH BARROW GOLD LOZENGE

THE TECHNOLOGICAL SKILL and mathematical precision evidenced in the construction of the great prehistoric monuments of the British Isles and Europe has always been cause for wonder. Many of these monuments, such as Stonehenge, Avebury, Callanish and the Ring of Brodgar, which are generally taken to be ceremonial sites, are clearly the work of architects, supervised by a rich and settled aristocracy dominated by astronomer-priests of the type of the later Druids.

Normanton Down, Wiltshire, half a mile south of Stonehenge, is one of the finest barrow cemeteries in Britain. The remarkable

Bush Barrow was excavated in 1808. Eleven feet (3.4 meters) high, the mound covered the grave of a man of considerable height and high social standing. He was clearly a chieftain or a king. He had been buried in his raiment, and on his breast had been sewn a remarkable lozenge-shaped gold breastplate, with an engraved surface. The suggested date for the burial is 1900 B.C.

It is assumed that the lozenge (now in the Devizes Museum, Wiltshire), is a calendar, though its fragile nature would seem to make it impractical for regular use on the site (Stonehenge). If it is indeed a calendar, it was probably specially fashioned for ritual or deposition—an object of beauty created for the gods. The everyday equivalent used for practical purposes could have been of leather or perhaps of wood. The lozenge seems to have been a device employed to ascertain the dates of the year, leap years, solar equinoxes, solstices and the rising and setting of the moon. The pattern was a set

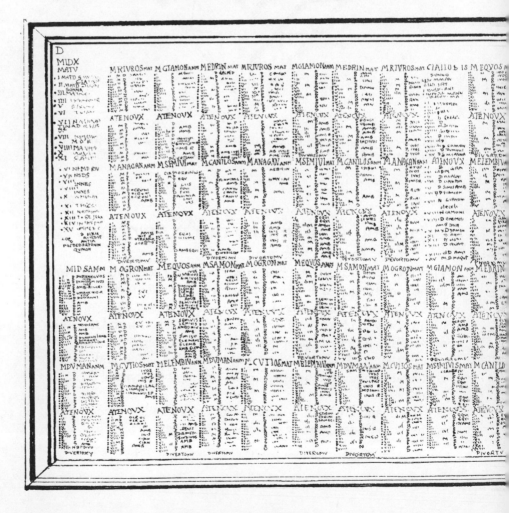

of "sight" lines and was accurate to within a third of a day per year. It demonstrates beyond doubt an advanced knowledge of mathematics and astronomy.

The Bush Barrow "calendar" takes note of the summer and winter solstices, and also marks the "quarter" days that were of such importance in the Celtic year—Halloween (Samain), Candlemas, (Imbolc), May Day (Beltain) and Lammas (Lughnasa).

The Coligny calendar was an engraved plate of bronze measuring about five feet wide by about three feet high, with a molded bronze frame attached at the edges by rivets. This is an impression of the calendar be-

fore it was broken. The sixteen lists of months were divided from each other by lines of small holes, one beside each day, running vertically up and down the plate. The holes weakened the metal and, at some stage in its history, it was broken into some two hundred pieces of which about half were found toward the end of the nineteenth century.

The calendar is among the oldest inscriptions in a Celtic language yet known. Roman numbers and letters are used, but the arrangement of the calendar and the words are Celtic—probably the work of Gaulish Druids just before or just after the beginning of the Christian era.

Coligny lies in wooded country beside the source of the Solnan River, a tributary of the Saône, fifteen miles northeast of Bourg-en-Bresse, Ain, France. The calendar is now in the Musée de la Civilisation Gallo-Romaine, Lyon. The illustration on page 139 shows the two complete months which can be assembled from seven pieces originally forming part of the fourth column of the calendar. The months are SAMON-, a month of thirty days, designated as *mat*, good; and DUMAN-, twenty-nine days, designated *anm*, not good.

Ritual shafts in Britain (places for ritual and druidic deposition) in some cases predate those found on the continent. Close by, there is a remarkable example at Wilsford, on Normanton Down, dug circa 1200 B.C. that reaches a depth of more than one hundred feet (thirty meters). Another at Swanwick, Hampshire, dating from roughly the same period, is twenty-four feet (7.3 meters) deep; when it was excavated, a wooden post, some five feet (1.5 meters) high, was found at the bottom, around which were traces of flesh and blood.

The tradition of offering into pits or shafts in the ground is a further indication of the antiquity of druidism in Britain. Stonehenge, with its surrounding "ritual" landscape, is unique. Perhaps it was thought to be the dwelling of some great god—a universal god such as Belenos, with his clear solar affinities. It has been concluded that, apart from serving as a temple for the god, Stonehenge functioned as a type of astronomical computer, employing a base of nineteen years to bring solar and lunar years into synchronization. We know that this was the system used by the Druids.

Some connection between the Bronze Age astronomer-priests and the Druids of the historical period seems to be supported by the Coligny calendar. This fascinating document is drawn up in sixteen columns of months covering a period of five years, each month divided into two parts by the insertion of the recognizably Celtic word *Atenoux*. *Noux*, "night(s)," has its equivalent in the Gaelic *nocht* or Welsh *nos*. *Atenoux* means something like "the returning night(s)," "renewal."

The Coligny calendar was not only lunar, in which case the month is divided into two periods corresponding to the waxing and waning of the moon, but luni-solar. This means that the Druids tried to square the system of the lunar months with the solar year. The fact that the calendar covers a period of five years gives credence to Diodorus's statement that the continental Celts held quinquennial sacrifices, and five was an important number in Celtic numerology.

The Gauls called themselves the "sons of the god of night," and defined the seasons in terms not of days, but of nights. The year began with the month called *Samon* (cognate with *Samain*). Giamon was the first month of summer. These months were held to be periods of intense supernatural power, both destructive and beneficial.

THE ENIGMA OF DURRINGTON WALLS

THE DRUIDS, then, were part of the rich fabric of Celtic life, and their power and influence extended far beyond the religious sphere. But where are the traces of druidism today? We know that their temples were in groves and that scarcely any trace of them remains. Physical evidence must be sought, rather, in their schools. This means reinterpreting several perplexing archaeological survivals, the foremost of which is Durrington Walls, Wiltshire.

There is very little to see at Durrington Walls nowadays. Much of the 25-acre (10.1-hectare) site has been plowed and is visible only in aerial photographs. It consists of an enclosure surrounded by a huge, flat-bottomed perimeter ditch. The chalk excavated from this ditch was piled up into a bank *outside* it, indicating non-defensive use. Excavation of the ditch (in the late 1960s) revealed massive deposits of domestic rubbish—ash, broken animal bones, pottery shards, flints—concentrated at two entrances. Two series of concentric postholes were found, both set deeply into the chalk. Archaeologists concluded that they were the remains of very large circular buildings with steeply pitched timber roofs, probably thatched and with central smoke holes.

It has been suggested that Durrington Walls housed the builders and priests of nearby Stonehenge. Its sheer size, and non-defensive nature, hints at a special use—or use by special people. A further clue was provided by analysis of the many animal bones found among the refuse. There are indications that, instead of animals being butchered at the site, choice cuts were brought there—as offerings to an elite population? Pork seems to have been the meat most commonly eaten, and the Celtic aristocracy is known to have had a passion for pork.

Durrington Walls is close to the River Avon, and to the strange site of Woodhenge, which excavation showed to have been an isolated, circular building with a ground plan similar to that of the Durrington huts. At Woodhenge, the remains of a sacrificed child were found.

Most Iron Age Celtic sites in Britain are, unlike Durrington Walls, hilltop strongholds and tribal centers, such as the massive Maiden Castle in Dorset or Danebury Rings in Hampshire. Several major hillforts occur in Dorset, which was overwhelmed in the first years of the Roman conquest by Vespasian. The hand of the conqueror fell heavily: the defenses of the hillforts were despoiled, and their populations moved out; the whole area was laced with Roman roads, forts, camps and towns. Scarcely twenty miles (thirty-two kilometers) northwest of Maiden Castle, however, one of the most spectacular hillforts in Dorset seems strangely to have escaped the conqueror's lethal attention. This hillfort is Pilsdon Pen.

PILSDON PEN:
A DRUIDIC SANCTUARY

PILSDON PEN is the highest point—910 feet (277 meters)—in Dorset. It is a long, blunt ridge at the culmination of a ring of steep hills around the lush pastures of Marshwood Vale, which runs down toward Bridport, a few miles southward. Some twenty years ago the former owner of the site, Michael Pinney, was instrumental in arranging an excavation. Although the excavation was never completed, its preliminary findings were startling.

The fort has two incomplete ramparts just below the crest of the hill; on the southwest side is a wide gateway and through this leads the so-called "sacred way." These ramparts enclose an oval area of about ten acres (four hectares), a modest size compared with most Dorset hillforts. Aerial photography revealed the plan of a large rectangular building close to the center of the fort. This was shown to be timber-framed and of unusual construction, not only in being rectangular but also in containing a deep posthole with a ramp for a sizable ritual pole or tree. Traces of circular huts, the traditional Iron Age design, were identified by one of the entrances, and in addition to a considerable amount of domestic debris there were intriguing remains of a crucible and fragments of gold. A much larger horseshoe-shaped hut structure was also identified, the construction and purpose of which appeared to be similar to that of the rectangular enclosure.

The Iron Age date was fixed by finds of pottery and a gold coin of the Suessiones, but the discovery of a single ballista bolt demonstrated that Pilsdon Pen was used into the early Roman period. A collection of sling stones, buried in the foundations of one of the huts, was the only token of defense, suggesting that for some reason the Romans never attacked the site.

So what was Pilsdon Pen? The excavator, Peter Gelling, suggests that the two central buildings were part of a temple complex. Given a pre-Roman date, any temple must be ascribed to the Druids. As in the case of Durrington Walls, the presence of domestic refuse argues for an occupation site, and there is a clear similarity in that the refuse heap is far removed from the central building. There was something significant about the building and whoever lived in it in both cases: at Pilsdon the hilltop was of enormous strategic significance, commanding the Marshwood Vale and the approaches to Lyme Bay, but it had defenses that were not even finished. If its strategic importance was not exploited, what are we to make of it?

We visited Pilsdon Pen on a glorious day late in November 1987 to seek an answer. Climbing the steep slopes in the early morning we stood on the top of the ramparts and looked down the mist-enshrouded Marshwood Vale toward Lyme Bay. There was no feeling of an armed camp or tribal center; instead, we felt that this eminence had been chosen for its solitude and sweeping views of the world. We pondered what aspect of druidic practice might have been located here. The intuitive answer seemed plain: if it was not a temple, it must have been a *school*.

The fascination of Pilsdon Pen does not end at the hilltop. To the south, hidden behind Sliding Hill, stands Bettiscombe Manor, which dates from the fourteenth century. The house is steeped in legends: the most spectacular is that of the "screaming skull" of Bettiscombe—which is said to scream if taken from the manor house. The skull, of Iron Age date, is of a woman probably in her early thirties. It is likely that it was brought down to the house from a spring high up on Sliding Hill. The glassy texture of the skullcap gives an appearance of mineral absorption consistent with immersion in a spring and medical examination indicates damage to the bone consistent with septicemia, which may have accompanied a fatal wound. The implication that the Bettiscombe woman suffered ritual death has unmistakable Celtic and druidic overtones.

It is possible that the manor and village of Bettiscombe originally formed the site of a Celtic shrine, deep in the dense oakwoods of Marshwood Vale. Shortly after Domesday, Bettiscombe is recorded as belonging to the Benedictine Monks of St. Stephen's in

Caen. There is an indication that the Benedictines founded a chapel on the site of the present church and village as a focus for their attempts to Christianize the entrenched Celtic paganism of the northern end of Marshwood Vale under the shadow of Pilsdon Pen.

The closeness of the sea and the presence in medieval times of the monks from Normandy, led us to wonder whether in the tumultuous years of Caesar's conquest of Gaul, or during the Claudian proscription of druidism, members of the order fled here from Gaul, finding their way through the dense oakwood toward the sanctuary on the high place of the Pen.

CELTS
AND GERMANS

THE CELTIC LANDS lay on the northern and western borders of the classical world; the Germans inhabited the northern wilderness beyond. These densely forested German homelands did not come into direct contact with the classical Greek sphere of influence which was limited essentially to the Mediterranean coast and its immediate eastern hinterland in southeastern Europe and modern Anatolia. Roman contact with the Germans began only when the boundaries of the empire were pushed northward through Gaul and reached the natural barrier of the Rhine. Despite strenuous efforts by the early emperors to advance farther, that was where the Roman frontier was eventually consolidated.

The boundaries between Celt and German, however, were often diffuse. Caesar noted that on the northern Gaulish frontier some tribes he classified as Celtic were reputed to be Germans who had intermingled with the Celts during one of their southerly migrations. Classical writers' descriptions suggest essentially similar heroic warrior societies. There were differences between them, but they were of degree rather than kind. The semi-nomadic German tribal system was less evolved than the settled agricultural Celtic system based upon fortified strongpoints. And the pan-tribal druidic caste of the Celts seems to have had no parallel in the Germanic pagan priesthood, although the similarities between the Celtic and Germanic pantheons and religious practices were strong.

We learn from Tacitus, for example, that the elected German kings were also priests, and exercised religious power. This combination of druidic rank and kingship is also encountered among the Celts. The Germanic system, however, seems to have been less structured, almost as if it showed the Celtic system in an embryonic form.

As heroic societies based upon a primitive agriculture that resulted in nomadic wanderings from one forest clearing to another, the German tribes flourished by raiding their settled neighbors, whether Celtic, Roman or German. The booty from such raiding sustained the warrior elite by providing a treasury of fine ornaments, armor and weapons from which the king could reward the prowess of his nobles and followers.

According to Tacitus, it was quite common for German raiders to dedicate all their booty to the war gods. This dedication applied not only to costly and valuable weapons and armor but also to animals and to captives who could otherwise have been sold very profitably into slavery. The Germans sometimes went to extraordinary lengths to sacrifice expensive articles of war and commerce, deliberately breaking them up before dedicating them. Often they would deposit them as offerings in pools or streams, a practice strongly reminiscent of Celtic ritual.

The similarities between the Celtic and Germanic pantheons and the ritual offerings to these gods are so close that it is possible that the two races were closely related. The classical authors describe both Celtic and Germanic warriors as tall, large-framed and of fair or ruddy complexion. The Celtic and Germanic worlds evolved alongside each other in prehistoric Europe, and their languages, religions, customs and social organization were similar. Geographical proximity alone makes it likely that much agricultural experience was common to them both. That would have given rise to similar religious systems based upon the four distinct phases of the northern agricultural year and the experience of a similar European topography—one dominated by a heavily forested landscape that had to be cleared for farming. Tree worship was a fundamental religious feature of both cultures.

CELTIC INFLUENCE IN GERMANIA

MANY BOG BODIES that invite comparison with Lindow Man have been found in Denmark. Any discussion of Celtic influence or presence there must take account of the Gundestrup caldron, an unmistakably Celtic silver bowl found in a small peat bog in Himmerland, northern Jutland, in 1891. It carries highly characteristic reliefs depicting scenes from Celtic mythology and life. The caldron was carefully broken up into its constituent plates and base before being deposited in Raevemose, once part of the larger Borremose where bog bodies were found in the 1940s. Most scholars tend to the view that the caldron originated in the Celtic east, probably in Dacia, in modern Romania. We feel, however, that the Gaulish influence in its design and workmanship is stronger. It is generally thought that the caldron made its long journey across Europe through trade, or as booty, before being deposited in the bog.

The Celts excelled at working metal and enamel; indeed, their technology far outstripped that of Rome. They dedicated their finest costliest craftsmanship to the gods, threw priceless weapons and ornaments into lakes, pools and wells. Some of the most famous Celtic objects—such as the Battersea shield and the Waterloo helmet, found in the mid-nineteenth century and now in the British Museum—have been found in the Thames in or near London. The huge lake deposit at Llyn Cerrig Bach, on Anglesey, is another spectacular example of cumulative votive offering. Many of the objects are of such elaborate workmanship that they were probably made specially to be cast into the waters for the gods. Today, this part of the pagan Celtic heritage persists in the habit of throwing coins into fountains or pools "for luck."

Why was such an undeniably Celtic object found so close to three Danish bog bodies? Were Celts and Germans mingled in prehistoric Denmark? Besides the enigmatic caldron, there is other material evidence of a Celtic presence. Some third-century B.C. Celtic chain mail was found in a peat bog at Hjortspring, together with a canoe measuring fifty-eight feet (eighteen meters) in length. Close by, there were other Celtic items, such as long wooden shields and iron-headed spears of a similar date. They seem to have been deposited in a pool, like artifacts from other important Celtic sites such as Llyn Cerrig Bach, in Anglesey, and La Tène, on Lac de Neuchâtel, in Switzerland.

Another caldron was found in recent years in eastern Jutland, at Brå, near Horsens. This was a great bronze vessel, adorned with Celtic animal motifs in the La Tène style. It had been broken into fragments like the Gundestrup caldron, and deposited in a small pit in the ground, undoubtedly as a votive deposit. It seems to us that its origin lies farther east than that of the Gundestrup caldron, probably in Bohemia or Moravia in modern Czechoslovakia, and it was probably brought to Denmark along the River Elbe. All these finds point away from the Germanic dedication of booty to the gods, and indicate typically Celtic offering.

The indications are that the Celts exerted some cultural influence on the Germanic peoples in the late prehistoric period, although the nature and extent of this are by no means clear. It has been suggested by some eminent archaeologists that there are cogent arguments for the presence of a Celtic aristocracy or overlordship in some areas of the Germanic countries, which would involve an attendant druidic priesthood; this idea fits neatly into our picture.

CELTIC STONE HEADS
AND HOLY WELLS IN DENMARK

MANY UNMISTAKABLY Celtic stone heads are found built into the walls of Danish medieval churches. A three-faced head, with typically Celtic features and pronounced triangular motifs, was found in a gravel pit at Glejbjerg, in South Jutland. A single-faced head was buried beneath it. This latter appears to have been the keystone in a doorway or window arch of an old building. Another three-faced head, from the manor house at nearby Bramminge Kirke, also has triangular Celtic features, and is noteworthy in possessing a torque, a quintessential Celtic ornament. It is, of course, possible that these heads came to Denmark through trade or booty, but that is less likely than in the case of the Gundestrup caldron, for they are extremely heavy and of doubtful aesthetic value for a Germanic barbarian raider. It is highly likely that they were built into obscure corners of churches with their obvious pagan attributes hidden.

Holy wells and sacred groves of typically Celtic character are associated with the ancient churches of Denmark. At Bramminge Kirke, the church stands in a grove of oaks and there is a strong tradition that there is a holy well on the site. A clear example of a

Celtic holy well is situated at Rorkaer, close to the Danish-German border. The name means "pond of reeds," and the well is in a field named Heliggaard-Fenner ("enclosure of holy water"). The holy well at Vestervig, in northern Jutland, is in the grounds of the parish church. The church is dedicated to St. Thager, who traditionally brought Christianity to Denmark, but the Celtic origins of the well are shown by the relief carvings of stone heads in and around the church and the proximity of an Iron Age settlement to the north.

The upper part of a wooden figure found in a bog, Broddenbjerg-mose, Asmild, Viborg, Jutland, Denmark; the lower part of the figure is smeared with a thick layer of resin.

The word Lvgos carved, together with a stylized beast, on a tombstone at Tømmerby Kirke, Thy, Jutland, Denmark.

THE TOMMERBY STELA

In the church at Tømmerby Kirke in Denmark are two carved stone slabs (stelae) that display strongly Celtic features in their carving, but one of them has characteristics that straddle the cultures. The figure on one of them has Celtic features, and holds in its outstretched hand a cross with equal arms, similar in style and shape to Irish examples. Alongside the cross is a curious inscription in a mixture of Irish and Latin script, interposed with Runic features. The inscription translates "God's right hand." On the opposite side of the stela is a five-letter inscription that is difficult to decipher because of its location, but seems to read: "Lugos." There is also a carved motif of a lynx, one of the animals associated with this important Celtic god.

All these clues fit readily into the Danish Iron Age. This, by definition, stretches into the historical Danish period, which commenced in about the fifth century A.D. There is no evidence for a Celtic influx into Denmark during this period. On the contrary, by the fifth century, Germanic migration into the collapsing Roman

Empire was in full flood, and Celtic migration from Britain was southward and not into any part of Germany.

If the Celtic influences are associated primarily with sacred groves or holy wells, could they be relics of an elite Celtic priesthood in the midst of the prehistoric Danes? Was the prehistoric Danish priesthood *Celtic*?

The Celts and the Germans established fundamentally different types of agricultural settlements: the Celtic system was usually focused around a permanent single homestead in a forest clearing, whereas the Germanic system favored a simple village of a transient character. Tacitus reminds us that the Germans had little patience with organized agriculture and would readily move from site to site as the fertility of the ground was exhausted. It is therefore possible that two distinct cultural groupings, sharing many basic similarities, emerged over the centuries, and we may now be finding traces of Celtic "islands" grouped around sacred sites deeply buried in the midst of the Germanic system.

THE BORREMOSE MYSTERY

NOT ALL the Danish bog bodies are as well preserved as Tollund Man. Neither do they all bear the hallmarks of sacrificial death. With those that are well preserved we can distinguish a category of executed bodies; Tacitus notes that for certain crimes, such as adultery and sodomy, the malefactors were punished by being pinioned in lakes or marshes with sticks and stones. Many Danish bog bodies seem to come into this execution category. One was an adolescent girl who had not only been pinioned but had her head shaved as well. Her death seems to have been caused directly by drowning. Several severed heads have also been found in peat bogs in Jutland and North Germany. While there is a possibility of sacrificial deposit in some cases, in others the evidence is ambiguous and death could have resulted from execution.

Can the Danish bodies illuminate the death of Lindow Man? On the evidence of their finely manicured hands and fingernails, it has been suggested that the sacrificial victims were aristocratic. The lack of plants in flower in their last meals indicates that the sacrifices took place in winter or spring. Possibly they were sacrificed to

Nerthus, the earth goddess—one of the most powerful German deities—to ensure fertility.

There is a strong body of evidence, supported by legends, that the goddess was ritually paraded around the fields in springtime and that her acolytes and consort were ritually slaughtered after the ceremony. The evident aristocracy of Tollund Man and Grauballe Man might be explained by assuming that they were the sacrificed priests of the earth mother. But, if their deaths had merely seasonal significance, why have we not found more sacrificial bodies?

An interesting difference between the burial of Lindow Man and the Danish bodies, which may throw some light on the significance of the Danish deaths, is that Lindow Man was deposited in a pool in the peat, as were the two caldrons. The Danish bodies, however, were placed in *old peat cuttings*. There is therefore a sense of *burial* rather than of votive offering. The use of old work surfaces (peat was presumably exploited by the prehistoric Danes for fuel or agricultural use) might indicate not only the dark, moist embrace of the earth mother, but the *knowledge* that peat had preservative properties.

Borremose covers a wide area near the village of Lille Bind-erup. An Iron Age village stood on an island at the southern end of the fen. This has been excavated to reveal the postholes and timber frame impressions of a cluster of wooden longhouses, grouped about a paved causeway that winds across the bog to the center of the island. The first-century-B.C. village was built upon substantial third-century-B.C. foundations, surrounded by a deep defensive ditch and inner rampart. The paved causeway was sunk below the flooded surface of the fen and flanked by deep ditches so that only the initiated could gain entrance. This stronghold bears more resemblance to a Celtic-defended homestead than anything else that has come down to us from the Danish prehistoric period.

Three bodies were recovered from Borremose between the years 1946 and 1948. No further bodies have been found there, despite intensive searches. The first was found near the remains of the village. It was some six feet deep in the bog, enclosed in a soft deposit resting upon very solid peat strewn with birch branches. The excavators and laborers identified this natural tomb as an ancient peat working overgrown with birch and then filled in during the last two millennia. The body was that of a man, probably dating from the first century B.C. (when the village was last occupied). He was buried in a cross-legged sitting position, although the original posture was obscured by the enormous compression of the peat.

Borremose Man's state of preservation was very good. He was shorter in stature than Lindow Man; one of his eyes still retained enough of the eyeball to discern a black iris and his finely formed hands were taken as indicating aristocratic status. His sacrificial death was pinpointed by the three-stranded hempen rope around his neck, and by the remains of a vegetable cereal in his stomach that closely resembled the last meals of Tollund Man and Grauballe Man. The rope was just over a meter long, neatly stitched at each end to prevent unraveling, and fastened by a slipknot. Borremose Man's head was sharply twisted to the left, although it is not clear whether this was from compression by the peat or from the breaking of his neck by hanging. The presence of the rope around his neck, with its slipknot, could just as easily have implied strangulation. (The rope around Tollund Man's neck was made of two braided leather strips, rather than hemp, and knotted into a simple noose. Although there were no dislocated or broken bones in his neck, the presence of the noose was a clear indication that Tollund Man had been hanged rather than strangled.)

Borremose Man did have further injuries, which seemed to have accompanied or preceded his death. His right femur was broken just above the knee, and the back of his skull was broken. He had suffered a *triple death*. The crushing of the back of his skull would certainly have killed him, but it was followed by hanging and drowning in the peat. As in the cases of other bog bodies, a leg was broken, perhaps in deliberately rough treatment before death or to prevent his spirit walking after death.

As with Lindow Man, the strangulation seems to have been the *coup de grâce*. And, again like Lindow Man, Borremose Man seems to have come naked to the resting place, although he had two sheepskin capes—one with a collar that could be buttoned at the neck—rolled up at his feet. Across the body was a birch branch over a yard (one meter) long.

The clear sacrificial nature of Borremose Man's triple death is not matched by the other bodies from the fen. Neither are as well preserved, both are women and both date from the same time as the sacrificed man and the Iron Age village. The first was found in 1947, 1,100 yards (one kilometer) to the north of the man's body. She lay face downward on a sheet of birch bark in an ancient peat excavation, with three short sticks across her back. Much of her body had been destroyed or crushed beyond recognition, presumably by compression of the peat. Her hair was short, perhaps cropped just before death, and she wore an amber bead and bronze disk on a leather strap around her neck. The upper part of her body was naked and the lower half was covered by pieces of material: a blanket and a shawl were discerned in addition to several pieces of woolen cloth. Her right leg, like that of the man, had been broken before her death, although this time the fracture was just below the knee rather than above it. A collection of small bones alongside her body indicated the presence of a baby who had shared her fate. The prone posture, the arrangement of sticks and the absence of any evident cause of death other than the implication of drowning suggested that this was an execution, probably for adultery, in keeping with the observations of Tacitus.

The second Borremose woman, discovered in 1948, was long-haired. She, too, was found in an old peat cutting, just south of the man and the Iron Age village, and like the first woman she lay face downward. Her right arm was bent up against her face, her left leg bent beneath her with the left arm underneath. Her body was covered with a large blanket, fitted with a strap for it to double as a skirt. Again, there was no obvious cause of death, which must be inferred as due to drowning, although she had suffered a brutal scalping of the back of her head and her face had been crushed. Again, an execution seems more likely than a ritual death, although no sticks or pinions were found.

The bodies were found at widely separate places in the bog, which does not argue for a simple killing site. Nevertheless, the botanical and geological evidence indicates that the deaths were contemporary with the first-century-B.C. village. The assumption must be that the three victims lived in the village. Could these supposedly simple Iron Age peasants have been associated with such a magnificent artifact as the Gundestrup caldron, deposited at the northern extremity of Borremose?

Like the other typically Celtic offerings already discussed, the caldron is an isolated deposit. It was placed at the edge of the bog, just beneath a slight eminence that overlooks the expanse of the fen. It is tempting to link the caldron with the village. Was that village, perhaps, the settlement of a Celtic priesthood? Could Borremose be the Celtic site we are looking for in prehistoric Denmark? And was

Borremose Man, like Lindow Man, a Druid who suffered a triple death as a special offering to the gods?

The finding of a triple death and the Gundestrup caldron near an untypical defended village in the midst of Borremose raises perplexing questions. The triple death of the man finds its echo in the presence of three bodies, just as Lindow Man is flanked by the skull of Lindow Woman and the fragmentary remains of Lindow Man II. The motif of the *triple* places the Celtic fingerprint on both sites.

Acknowledgments

For permission to publish, we are grateful to the following individuals and institutions: The photograph of Lindow Moss, Richard Blower; the photographs of Lindow Man reproduced by courtesy of the British Museum; the excavation site, R. C. Turner; the photographs of Cernunnos, the Celtic god, from the Gundestrup caldron, Jutland, Denmark, the National Museum, Copenhagen, Denmark; the photographs of gold torque, Snettisham, Norfolk, reproduced by courtesy of the British Museum; photograph of torques, Libenice, Bohemia, Czechoslovakia, Alena Rybova and Bohumil Soudsky, Ceskoslovensak Akademic Ved, Praha; photograph of wooden tricephalos in Llandinam Church, Monmouthshire, W. J. Hemp, 1956, Montgomeryshire Collection LIV:2; photograph of three-headed torso, Condat, Dordogne, France, Musée des Beaux-Arts, Bordeaux, France; photograph of stone head of the one-eyed god, Balor, Christie's, London; photograph of bronze shield from the River Thames at Battersea, London, by courtesy of the British Museum; photographs of Celtic stone heads in Chester, Cheshire and Glossop, Derbyshire, the Manchester Museum; photograph of Celtic stone head, Wilmington, East Sussex, E. W. Holden, Steyning, West Sussex; photographs of Celtic god, Euffigneix, Haute-Marne, France, Musée des Antiquités Nationales, Yvelines, France; photograph of bronze model cult-wagon, Strettweg, Austria, Landesmuseum Joanneum, Graz, Austria; photograph of the Antler Dance, Abbots Bromley, Adam Woolfitt; photograph of a Dressed Well, Saddleworth, Lancashire, Anthony Myers Ward; photographs of a male nude figure and bronze Gallo-Roman horse, Rudiobus, from Neuvy-en-Sullias, Orléans, Musée Historique.

The line drawings have been derived and adapted from numerous published sources: Siberian tattooed skin, page 24, Rudenko, I., 1970; Taranis, page 46, from a photograph by the Musée des Antiquités Nationales, France; Esus, page 48, from a photograph by Landesmuseum, Trier, Luxembourg; Teutates, page 48, and Broddenbjerg Man, page 161, from the photographs by the National Museum, Copenhagen; bronze Druid figure, page 51, from a photograph by Musée Historique, Orléans, France; bronze Celtic priest figurine, page 85, from a photograph by H. J. M. Green; Alpraham altars, page 110, from photographs by R. W. Feachem of altars on loan from Anita Sebastian; torques and garrote, page 113, from photographs by the British Museum, London, and Ard-Mhúsaem na h-Eireann, Baile atha Cliath, Ireland; triskele bronze decoration, page 131, Kenner, H., 1956, 36; Esus and Tarvos Trigaranus, pages 136 and 137, Espérandieu, E., 1911, IV, 214; extract from the Coligny Calendar, page 139, and impression of calendar, pages 150–51, from photographs by Musée de la Civilisation Gallo-Romaine, Lyon, France; Sucellos, page 142, Reinach, S., 1905, 266; Ogam alphabet, page 142, various sources and Ross, A., 1986, 99; probable Druid on stone relief, page 146, Espérandieu, E., 1915, V,

217; bear, page 147, from a photograph by the Museum of Antiquities, The University, Newcastle upon Tyne, England; Bush Barrow gold plaque, page 149, from a photograph by the Wiltshire Archaeological and Natural History Society Museum, Devizes, Wiltshire, England; Lugos stela, page 162, from a photograph by the late Dr. Erling Rump.

The maps have been derived and compiled from various published sources including the following: the location of Lindow Moss, page 10, various sources and Stead, I., *et al.*, 1986; Gaul at the time of Julius Caesar, page 19, including Cunliffe, B., 1988, 92–105; the Hallstatt world, page 144, and the La Tène world, page 56, selections derived from Megaw, J. V. S., 1970; Kruta, V., 1978; Powell, T. G. E., 1980; Ross, A., 1986; Cornovia, page 61, various and Webster, G., 1975; Denmark, page 66, including Glob, P. V., 1969; Ross, A., 1986; Borremose, page 67, extract from Geodaetisk Institut map Denmark 1:25,000 Np 1216 II NW, Ars; Thorvildsen, E., and Kehler, S., 1963, 252–59; Cornovia, page 76, Hibernia and Britannia, page 80, and British and Roman sites, page 93, extracts from Ordinance Survey *Map of Southern Britain in the Iron Age*, 1962 (Chessington); Webster, G., 1975; Frere, S. S., *et al.*, 1987; Gallia, page 83, various and Rivet, A. L. F., 1988; the Gold Route, pages 108–109, and the Wicklow Mountains, page 118, various and S. O. $^1/_2$-inch sheet 18, Dublin; territory of the Durotriges, page 123, including O. S. *Map of Southern Britain in the Iron Age*, 1962 (Chessington); Cunliffe, B., 1974; Agache, R., *et al.*, 1983.

Bibliography

Agache, R. *et al.*, *Tabvla Imperii Romani: Condàte-Lvtetia*, London, 1983.

Alexander, M., *British Folklore, Myths and Legends*, London, 1982.

Barrett, W. H., *Tales from the Fens*, London, 1963.

Bethel, D., *Cheshire*, London, 1979.

Biel, J., "The Late Hallstatt chieftain's grave at Hochdorf," *Antiquity 55*, 16–18, 1981.

Bowker, J., *Goblin Tales of Lancashire*, Lancaster, 1883.

Bradley, R., and Gordon, K., "Human skulls from the River Thames, their dating and significance," *Antiquity 62*, 503–509, 1988.

Briggs, K., *A Dictionary of Fairies*, London, 1976.

Bromwich, R., *Trioedd Ynys Prydein* (The Welsh Triads), Cardiff, 1979.

Brothwell, D., *The Bog Man and the Archaeology of People*, London, 1986.

Burl, A., *The Stone Circles of the British Isles*, London, 1976.

—— *The Rites of the Gods*, London, 1981.

Caesar, Gaius Julius: *see* Gardener, J. F.

Chadwick, N. K., "Early Literary Contacts between Wales and Ireland," in Moore, D. (ed.), *The Irish Sea Province in Archaeology and History*, Cardiff, 1970.

Chaney, W., *The Cult of Kingship in Anglo-Saxon England*, Manchester, 1975.

Collingwood, R. G., and Wright, R. P., *The Roman Inscriptions of Britain*, Oxford, 1965.

Cross, T. P., and Slover, C. H., *Ancient Irish Tales*, Dublin, 1969.

Cunliffe, B., *Iron Age Communities in Britain*, London, 1974.

—— *Greeks, Romans and Barbarians*, London, 1988.

Dudley, D. R., and Webster, G., *The Rebellion of Boudicca*, London, 1962.

Duffy, J., *Patrick in His Own Words*, Dublin, 1975.

Ellison, A., "A Native Roman and Christian Ritual Complex of the 1st Millennium AD: excavations at West Hill, Uley, 1977–9," *Committee for Rescue Archaeology in Avon, Gloucestershire and Somerset, Occasional Papers No. 9*, 305–28, 1979.

Espérandieu, E., *Recueil Général des Bas-Reliefs, Statues et Bustes de la Gaule Romaine*, Paris, 1907 I, 1908 II, 1910 III, 1911 IV, 1913 V, 1915 VI, 1918 VII, 1922 VIII, 1925 IX, 1928 X, 1938 XI, 1949 XIII, 1955 XIV, 1966 XV. Republished Farnborough, England, 1966.

Evans-Wentz, W. Y., *The Fairy Faith in Celtic Countries*, Oxford, 1911.

Feachem, R. W., "Medionemeton on the Lines of Antoninus Pius, Scotland," *Collection Latomus 103*, 210–16, 1969.

Fox, C., *A Find of the Early Iron Age from Llyn Cerrig Bach, Anglesey*, Cardiff, 1946.

——— *Pattern and Purpose*, Cardiff, 1958.

Frere, S. S., Rivet, A. L. F., and Sitwell, N. H. H., *Tabvla Imperii Romani: Britannia Septentrionalis*, London, 1987.

Gardener, J. F., *Caesar: The Conquest of Gaul* (translated by S. A. Handford), London, 1982.

Giraldus Canbrensis: *see* O'Meara, J. J.

Glob, P. V., *Jernaldermanden fra Grauballe*, Aarhus, 1959.

——— *The Bog People*, London, 1969.

Gowlett, J. A. V., Hedges, R. E. M., and Law, I. A. "Radiocarbon accelerator (AMS) dating of Lindow Man," in *Antiquity 63*, 71–79, 1989.

Gwynn, E., "The Metrical Dindshenchas," *Royal Irish Academy Todd Lecture Series XI*, Dublin, 1924.

Harris, A., *Human Measurement*, London, 1978.

Hatt, J. J., *The Ancient Civilization of the Celts and Gallo-Romans*, London, 1970.

Henderson, G., *Survivals in Belief among the Celts*, Glasgow, 1911.

Hobley, B., "An experimental reconstruction of a Roman Military turf rampart" (The Lunt, Baginton), *Roman Frontier Studies 1967*, 21–34, 1967.

Jackson, J., *Tacitus, The Annals, Books XIII-XVI*, London, 1981.

Jackson, K., *Language and History in Early Britain*, Edinburgh, 1953.

Jones, G., and Jones, T., *The Mabinogion*, London, 1975.

Kendrick, T., *The Druids*, London, 1928.

Kenner, H., "La civilisation et l'art celtique en Carinthie," in *OGAM VIII*, Pt 3, 21–38, Pl IV–XI, 1956.

Kinnes, I. A., *et al.*, "Bush Barrow Gold," in *Antiquity 62*, 24–39, 1988.

Kinsella, T., *The Táin*, Oxford, 1969.

Klindt-Jensen, O., *Denmark*, London, 1957.

——— *Gundestrupkedelen*, Copenhagen, 1961.

Kruta, V., *Les Celtes*, Paris, 1978.

Laing, L., *Celtic Britain*, London, 1979.

Le Roux, F., "Le calendrier gaulois de Coligny et la fête irlandaise de Samain," *OGAM IX*, Pts 5-6, 337–42, 1957.

Lewis, M. J. T., *Temples in Roman Britain*, Cambridge, 1966.

Macalister, R. A. S., *Tare: a Pagan Sanctuary of Ancient Ireland*, London, 1931.

——— *Corpus Inscriptionum Insularum Celticarum*, Dublin, 1945.

MacCana, P., *Celtic Mythology*, London, 1970.

MacCulloch, J. A., *The Religion of the Ancient Celts*, Edinburgh, 1911.

Mackie, E., *The Megalith Builders*, London, 1977.

MacNeill, M., *The Festival of Lughnasa*, Oxford, 1962.

Martin, M., *A Description of the Western Islands of Scotland* (a republication of the original of 1703, published in Stirling), London, 1934.

Mattingly, H., *Tacitus: The Agricola and The Germania*, London, 1970.

Megaw, J. V. S., *Art of the European Iron Age*, Bath, 1970.

Mommsen, Th., *Collectanea Rerum Memorabilium, by G. I. Solinus*, Berlin, 1958.

O'Cinneide, S., "Gaelic and the Druids," *A Journal of Irish Studies XII*, 119ff, 1977.

O'Curry, E., *Lectures on the Manuscript Materials of Ancient Irish History*, Dublin, 1878.

O'Grady, S. H., *Silva Gadelica*, London and Edinburgh, 1892.

Olmsted, G. S., "The Gundestrup Cauldron," *Collection Latomus 162*, 1979.

O'Meara, J. J., *Gerald of Wales: the History and Topography of Wales*, London, 1982.

O'Rahilly, C., *Táin Bó Cúalnge*, Dublin, 1967.

O'Rahilly, T. F., *Early Irish History and Mythology*, Dublin, 1946.

Oswald, A., and Gathercole, P. W., "Observations and excavation at Manduessedum," *Transactions of the Birmingham and Warwickshire Archaeological Society 74*, 30–52, 1956.

Pennant, T., *A Tour in Scotland; MDCCLXIX*, Warrington, 1774.

—— *A Tour in Scotland and Voyage to the Hebrides MDCCLXXII*, Chester, 1774.

—— *A Tour in Scotland MDCCLXXII Part II*, London, 1776.

Piggott, S., *Ancient Europe*, Edinburgh, 1965.

—— *The Druids*, London, 1974.

—— *The Earliest Wheeled Transport*, London, 1983.

Powell, T. G. E., *The Celts*, London, 1980.

Rees, A., and Rees, B., *Celtic Heritage*, London, 1967.

Reinach, S., *Cultes, Mythes et Religions*, Paris, 1905.

Renfrew, C., *Archaeology and Language*, London, 1988.

Richmond, I. A., *Roman Britain*, London, 1955.

Rivet, A. L. F., *Gallia Narbonensis*, London, 1988.

Rivet, A. L. F., and Smith, C., *The Place-Names of Roman Britain*, London, 1979.

Robins, D., Sales, K., and MacNeil, D., *Ancient Spins, Chemistry in Britain*, London, 1984, p. 283.

Robins, D., Sales, K., and Oduwole, D., "A Spin through the Past," *New Scientist 117*, 49, 1988.

Ross, A., *Pagan Celtic Britain*, London, New York, 1967.

—— "Pits, shafts and wells: sanctuaries of the Belgic Britons?" *Studies in Ancient Europe* (edited by J. M. Coles and D. D. Simpson), Leicester, 1968.

—— *Grotesques and Gargoyles* (text of book illustrated by and published under name of R. Sheridan), Newton Abbot, 1975.

—— *Folklore of the Scottish Highlands*, London, 1976a.

—— "Ritual Rubbish? The Newstead Pits," *To Illustrate the Monuments* (edited by J. V. S. Megaw), London, New York, 1976b.

—— "Chartres, the locus of the Carnutes," in *Studia Celtica XIV/XV*, 260–69 (edited by J. E. Caerwyn Williams), Oxford, 1980.

—— "Heads baleful and benign," *Between and Beyond the Walls* (edited by C. Burgess and R. Miket), Edinburgh, 1984.

—— *Druids, Gods and Heroes of Celtic Mythology*, London, 1986a.

—— *The Pagan Celts*, London, 1986b.

Ross, A., and Robins, D., "Face to Face with a Druid," *New Scientist 116*, 19, 1987.

Round, A. A., "Excavations at Wall, Staffordshire, on the site of the Roman forts

(Letocetum)," *Transactions of the South Staffordshire Archaeological and Historical Society*, XI, 7–31, 1970.

Rudenko, S. I., *Frozen Tombs of Siberia*, London, 1970.

Scott, J. M., *Boadicea*, London, 1975.

Selkirk, A., "Pilsdon Pen," *Current Archaeology 14*, 78–81, 1969.

Shell, C. A., and Robinson, P., "The Bush Barrow lozenge plate," in *Antiquity 62*, 248–60, 1988.

Simmons, I., and Tooley, M. (eds.), *The Environment in British Prehistory*, London, 1981.

Solinus, G. I., *see* Mommsen, Th., 1958.

Stead, J. M., *et al.*, *Lindow Man: the Body in the Bog*, London, 1986.

Stokes, W., *Sanas Cormaic*, Calcutta, 1868.

—————"The Rennes Dindshenchas" (with E. Windisch), in *Revue Celtique XV*, 272–336, 1895.

—————"Cóir Anman," in *Irische Texte III*, Leipzig, 1897.

Tacitus, C.: *see* Jackson, J., 1981, and Mattingly, H., 1970.

Thom, A. S., *Megalithic Sites in Britain*, Oxford, 1967.

Thom, A. S., Ker, J. M. D., and Burrows, T. R., "The Bush Barrow Gold Lozenge: is it a solar and lunar calendar for Stonehenge?" *Antiquity 62*, 492–502, 1988.

Thomas, C., *Exploration of a Drowned Landscape*, London, 1985.

Thorvildsen, E., and Kehler, S., *Med Arkaeologen Danmark Rundt*, Copenhagen, 1963.

Tierney, J. J., "The Celtic Ethnography of Posidonius," *Proceedings of the Royal Irish Academy 60 C5*, 189–275, 1960.

Todd, M., *The Coritani*, London, 1973.

—————*The Northern Barbarians*, London, 1975.

Webster, G., *The Cornovii*, London, 1975.

—————*The Roman Invasion of Britain*, London, 1980.

—————*Rome against Caratacus*, London, 1981.

—————*The British Celts and their Gods under Rome*, London, 1986.

White, K. D., *Greek and Roman Technology*, London, 1984.

Williams, I., *Pedeir Keinc Y Mabinogi*, Cardiff, 1930.

Index

Abbots Bromley, 108
Aberffraw, 122
Adonis, 72
Agricola, 77, 91, 127
Alderley Edge, 10, 60, 72–
  73, 95, 96, 98, 100, 104,
  106
Alpraham, 110–11
Andraste, 102, 119
Anglesey, 84, 86, 91–92,
  94, 96–97, 104, 106–7,
  108–12, 116, 120–23,
  124, 125, 133, 134, 148,
  159
Animal totemism, 68
Anker, River, 104
Anoniredi, 99
Antonine Wall, 127
Anu, 99, 105, 129
Aristotle, 141
Arlon, relief of possible
  Druid from, 146
Arnemetia, 129

Baal, sacrifices to, 37
Baginton, see Lunt
Balder, 72
Bard, 50, 131, 143
Barley bread, 32, 33
Battersea shield, 159
Bear, 145
Belenos, 35, 49, 152
Beltain, 13, 35, 41, 45, 67,
  71, 77, 91–92, 94–95, 99,
  101, 132–33, 151
Bettiscombe Manor, 155–
  156
    screaming skull at, 155
Black Annis, 105
Black Lake, 10, 60, 62, 70,
  71, 92, 95
Blood Brotherhood, 135
Boar, sacred, 63
    at Lindow Moss, 63
Bog bodies, burials, 12, 14,
  21, 22, 27, 29, 30, 41, 42,
  46, 66, 158–59, 163–67

Boggans, king, see Haxey
  hood game
Boggarts, 68, 69
Bogies, 68
Bollin River, 10, 61, 70, 74,
  97
Bonfires, 35–36, 77, 95–96
Borremose, 43, 66–68, 158–
  159, 163–67
Boudica, 87–91, 101–3, 106,
  114, 119, 121, 124–25
Brå caldron, 159–60
Bramminge Kirke, 160
Bread, barley, 32, 33, 71
    blackened, 12, 38
    burned, 13, 33, 67, 71
    unleavened, 14
Brentwood, Battle of, 81
Brigantia, 75, 85, 92, 124,
  129
Brigantes, 75, 80, 82, 102–
  103, 109
Brigit, 35, 107
Brigstock, 115
Britannia, 80, 81
Broddenbjergmose,
  wooden figure, 161
Brodgar, Ring of, 149
Bronze Age, 15, 23, 55, 64,
  96
Bruiden, 135
Bugganes, see Boggans,
  king
Bush Barrow gold calendar,
  149–51
Butser Hill Iron Age Farm,
  32

Caesar, Julius, 17, 19, 36,
  43, 44, 59, 65, 81–83, 84,
  132, 134, 135, 138, 140,
  144, 156
Caldron, Brå, 159–60
    Gundestrup, 48, 66,
  67, 136, 159–60, 166, 167
    Magic, Ritual, 98–99,
  122

Calendar festival, 13, 35
Callanish, 149
Camulodunum, 81, 82
Candlemass, see Imbolc
Caratacus, 81, 82, 84–85,
  88, 92, 103, 123
Carman, see Curragh
Carnuntum, 131
Cartimandua, 85, 102–3
Cattle Raid of Cooley, 135
Catus, 87–88, 92, 102, 114,
  119
Catuvellauni, 80, 109, 115
Celt, 18
Celtic, ancestor, see Dis
  Pater
    character, 54
    church, 146
    fringe, 18
    gold coins, 55
    hillforts, 55, 153–54
    identity, 59
    kings, 54
    stone heads, 107, 160,
  161
    world, 54, 56
Celts, Galatian, 134
    Insular, 42, 57
Cerne Abbas Giant, 59
Cernunnos, 59
Chariot, Place of the, see
  Mancetter
Cheshire, 61, 74, 75, 109
Chester, 10, 74–77, 91, 93,
  103, 106–7, 109, 127
Christmas, 35
Colchester, 81, 88
Coligny calendar, 138–39,
  150–51, 152
Collyweston, 115
Columba, St., 134
Conall Cernach, 138
Conchobar, King, 138
Corieltavi, 75, 76, 80, 81,
  109, 115
Corieltavia, 75
Cornovia, 61, 75, 81, 125

174

Cornovii, 74–75, 76, 80, 81, 84–89, 109
Crom Gruaich, 140
Crom Dubh, 108
Curragh, 133

Dagda, 59
Danebury Rings, 153
Dane Hills, 105–6
Deceangli, 75, 76, 80, 108
Dee, river, 61, 65, 75, 124
Denmark, 9, 15–16, 17, 19, 22, 23, 28, 29–30, 47, 66, 124, 142, 160–62
Derbyshire, 77, 107, 109, 116
Deva, see Chester
Devoted one, 37, 71–74, 91–92, 95–97, 99–100
Diet, Iron Age, 29–30
Dindshenchas, 140
Diodorus Siculus, 134, 144–45, 152
Diogenes Laertius, 141
Dis Pater, 59, 141
Diviciacus, 132, 143–44
Divine Victim, 71–74, 91–92, 97
Dobunni, 55, 76, 80
Dog, sacred, 53
Donn, 141
Dovaidona, 134
Druid, *passim* 50
    bronze representation, 51
    novitiate training, 53
Druidism, 34, 59, 133
Dublin, 108, 111, 118
Durotriges, 80, 123
Durrington Walls, 153–54, 155

Earith, Cambridgeshire, 85
East Anglia, see Iceni
Emain Macha, 135, 140
Erc, King, 134
Electron spin resonance (ESR), 14, 31, 33, 39
Esus, 45, 46, 47, 48, 57, 99, 135, 136

Filidh, 131
Fire festivals, Beltain, see Beltain
    Lughnasa, Samain, 35, 133, 141, 151
Fosse Way, 81, 88, 103–7, 114
Fox, fur armband, 53, 57–59, 125
    fur hat, 58, 126
    god, 54
    name applied to noblemen, 57

son of, see Lovernios tribe, 54
Fox, Sir Cyril, 122

Gaelic language, 147–48
Gallia, Gaul, 83, 84, 117, 132, 144, 148, 156
Gallic War, see Caesar, Julius
Garrote, 27, 47, 98, 113, 120
Germani, Germans, 47
Germanic gods, 47
    peoples, 157–58
Glejbjerg, 160
Gloucester, 88
Gold, route, 111–23, 149
Grauballe Man, 31, 39, 66, 67, 164, 165
Grenoside, see Sword Dancing
Groves, sacred, see *Nemet*-names
Gundestrup, see Caldron
Gwyr y Gogledd, see Men of the North
Gyrus, see Lunt

Hadrian's Wall, 127
Halloween, 151
Hallstatt, 58, 144
Handsworth, see Sword dancing
Haxey hood game, 69–70, 126
High Cross, 88–90, 94, 103–4, 106, 109, 114
Himmerland, 67, 159
Hjortspring, 159
Hochdorf, 58, 124
Holyhead, 103, 111
Holy Island, 111, 120, 121

Iceni, 80, 86–90, 114, 115, 117, 124
Imbolc, 35, 151
Insula sacra, 77, 97, 107, 124, 133
Invasion, Claudian, 81–82
    Julius Ceasar's, 81, 82–83
    Roman, 65, 81–83
Iona, 134
Ireland, 80, 96–97, 107, 111–12, 117, 122, 124–26, 132–38, 143, 147–48
Iron Age, 17, 30, 32, 64, 65, 126
    Danish, 17, 22, 28, 29–30, 47, 162

Kilguri, 74
King Alfred tale, 38

Lammas, 35, 151
Last meal, Grauballe Man, 31, 39, 41, 67, 163, 165
    Lindow Man, 12, 14, 29, 31, 34, 39, 41
    Tollund Man, 30, 31, 39, 41, 67, 163, 165
La Tène, 56, 112, 122, 124, 159
Leicester, 81, 105, 114
Leinster, 122
Letocetum, see Wall
Libenice, Czechoslovakia, 55
Lille Binderup, see Borremose
Lincoln, 81, 103
Lindow Common, 10, 62
    Man II, 128
    Moss, *passim* 9
    Woman, 11, 23, 127
Lleyn peninsula, 122
Llyn Cerrig Bach, 80, 120–123, 125, 159
London, 88–90, 114
Loarn, 57
Lovernianus, 54–55, 57
Lovernios, Lovernius, Lovernos,
    passim 53
Lugh, see Lugos
Lughnasa, 35, 133, 141, 151
Lugos, 35, 57, 108, 162
Lunt, 106–7, 109
Lydney, 55

Maeatae, 127
Maiden Castle, 123, 153, 154
Man, Isle of, 68, 77, 134, 148
Mancetter, Manduessedum, 90, 93, 94, 102–9, 114–15, 121, 124–125
Mannanan, 134
Mathgen, 145
May Day, see Beltain
May Eve, 38, 71
Maypole, 38
Menai Straits, 87, 109, 111, 123–25
Men of Art, see Druid
Men of the North, 74, 77
Mercury, 56–57, 116, 117
Mersey River, 10, 61, 65, 74–76, 82, 97, 124
Minerva, see Brigit
Mistletoe, druidic collection and use of, 40, 52, 138
    pollen in last meal, 40, 52

Mobberley, 10, 62, 71, 95–96, 98
Mona, see Anglesey
Mons Craupius, 127
Mound People, 23

Name, Naming, 59
Need-fire, 36
Nemet- (names, groves, sanctuaries), 80, 83, 94, 96, 160–61
Nero, Emperor, 86, 87
Nerthus, 99, 164
Neuvy-en-Sullias, France, 51
Ninth Legion, 89, 91, 103

Odin (Woden), 47
Ogam, 134, 143
Oran, 134
Ordovices, 80, 82, 84, 108
Ostorius Scapula, 85
Otherworld, Celtic, 35, 59, 135, 136–38

P Celtic, 148
Palynology, 63–65
Pancake, barley, 32, 33, 35, 71
    Beltain, 36, 37, 67
    sacred, 36, 96
Parisii, 80, 122
Paulinus, Suetonius, 86–91, 101–4, 106, 116, 121, 124
Pausaniaus, 134
Pazyryk tombs, 23, 24
Peat, 9, 17, 63, 164
Peat bog, preservation in, 21–25, 30, 41
Penkridge (Pennocrucium), 93, 107–9
Pete Marsh, Lindow Man, 12, 15
Picts, 127
Pilsdon Pen, 123, 135, 154–156
Pliny, 134
Pollen analysis, 17, 30, 63–65, 96
Prasutagus, 87–88, 92, 114, 117
Priest, 50, 84
Preservation,
    bodily, 21–25, 30, 41
    by desiccation, 23, 25
    natural, 21–22
    Pazyryk tombs, in, 23, 24
    peat bogs, in, 21–25, 30, 41
    by waterlogging, 21, 23
Pythagoras, 148

Q Celtic, 148

Radiocarbon dating, 9, 16, 63, 65, 67–68, 79, 127
Raevemose, 48, 67, 159
Ratae, see Leicester
Rhine, River, 19, 82, 124, 126
Riding the black lad, 73, 99
    the lord, 73, 97–100
Ritual death, 22, 27, 30, 65
    shafts, 152
Rorkaer, 161
Rostherne Mere, 70–71

Sacrifice, animal, 36, 44, 57
    human, 30, 36, 39, 43, 140
Saddleworth Moor, 23
St. Albans, 90, 103
St. Bees, knight preserved at, 41
St. John's day, 35
Samain, 35, 133, 141, 151, 152
Scotti, 127
Setantii, 76, 80, 108
Severn River, 61, 75, 76, 104, 107
Siberia, 23, 24
Silures, 76, 80, 82, 84, 85, 88, 90
Snettisham, torques of, 115, 117, 119
Snowdon, 85
South Shields, 147
Stone Age, Late, 96
    New, 64
Stonehenge, 149, 150, 154
Struan Micheil cake, 40
Sucellos, 59, 141, 142
Suetonius, see Paulinus, Suetonius
Swanwick shaft, 152
Sword dancing, 58, 126

Tacitus, 64, 87, 91, 102, 157–58, 163
Taltiu, 133
Tain Bó Cúailnge, 135
Tammuz, 72
Tara, 108, 113, 120, 133
Taranis, 36, 45, 46, 47, 98
Tarvos Trigaranus, 48, 135, 137
Teutates, 45, 46, 47, 48, 59, 99
Teutons, 43, 47
Thager, St., 161
Thetford, 115
Thistleton, 115
Thor, 47
Tiberius, Emperor, 84

Tlachtga, 133
Tollund Man, 28, 30, 31, 39, 41, 43, 66, 67, 120, 163–165
Tømmerby Kirke, 66, 162
Torque, 113, 114–20, 125
    Glascote, 113, 117
    Needwood, 113, 117
    Snettisham, 115, 117, 119
Trade Route, 114–24
Trent River, 61, 75, 76, 109
Trent-Severn passage, 107, 109
Trinovantes, 80, 88
Triple Death, 45, 49, 167
Triskele, 131

Uley, Gloucestershire, 55, 56
Uisnech, 133

Valley, 111, 121
Vates, 98–99, 131–32
Venonis, see High Cross
Vernemeton, 104–5, 107, 109, 115
Verulamium, see St. Albans
Vespasian, 82
Vestervig, 161
Vikings, 43, 47, 77
Vortigern, 134

Wall, 93, 107–9
Wallasey, 74
Waterloo helmet, 159
Water Newton, 115
Wash, 104, 116
Watling Street, 88–90, 94, 103–4, 106, 109, 111, 114
Weaver River, 10, 61, 75, 76
Well dressing, 77, 126
Wells sacred, 46, 53, 160–161
White Horse, 72, 73
Wicklow Hills, 108, 111, 118–19,121
Wild horse of Antrobus, 73
Willoughby-on-the-Wolds, see Vernemeton
Wilmslow, 10, 60, 61, 62, 72
Wilsford Shaft, 152
Winderby Girl, 67
Wirral, 74, 75
Woden (Odin), 47
Wolf, sacred, 53
Woodhenge, 153
Wroxeter, 93, 103, 109

York, 127